JULIE TROWELL

THE REAL WORLD REHAB

WHAT HAPPENS WHEN REHAB STOPS BEING POLITE...
AND RECOVERY STARTS GETTING REAL

For my "cuz" Brian

The only human I've ever seen bleed, cry, apologize,
and flirt all in the same five minutes.
But that was you,
broken but still charming,
hurting but still trying,
falling apart but still reaching for connection.
You fought longer than anyone knew.
You carried more than anyone understood.
Let these pages be the hand I wish I could've held
on the night you didn't stay.
And may your story live on
in every person who reads this
and chooses to stay one more day.

Contents

Preface

Rehab wasn't on my vision board. There was no candlelit epiphany or spiritual awakening that led me there. There was just a mess I could no longer outrun. The chaos, the lies, and the wreckage of good intentions finally caught up with me, and for the first time, I couldn't talk, charm, or numb my way out of it.

From the outside, it might look like I lost everything piece by piece. And I did: my marriage, my career, my home, and even my children for a time. But when everything else was stripped away, I finally found the one thing I had been missing all along: myself. Rehab is where that discovery began.

This isn't a recovery manual and it isn't a polished success story. It isn't clinical, sugar coated, or written to sound professional. This is the truth about treatment: the hesitation, the breakdowns, the belly laughs in the middle of the pain, and the quiet sacred moments when healing and humor first crack through the fear.

This isn't the *Malibu* version of rehab where your room comes with massages and a view of the ocean. This is the kind where group starts way too early, your roommate snores, and your *"scenic overlook"* is *Jerry* from group chain smoking in the courtyard.

But this is also the rehab that saves you. Not because it looks good on *Instagram*, but because it is real. Because honesty starts replacing denial. Because laughter lives right next to heartbreak. Because someone across the circle finally makes you feel less alone.

I have been on both sides, nurse and patient, and what I learned is simple: rehab saves lives because it is the place where rock bottom stops being the end and becomes the foundation.

Recovery is not about returning to who you used to be. It is about becoming someone you have never met before.

Welcome to *The Real World Rehab*.
    It is not about being polite.
    It is about getting real.

1

This Ain't the Hotel — It's Rehab (Lower Your Yelp Standards, Folks)

Rehab is not designed to be comfortable. It is designed to keep you from *dying*. If you walked in expecting aromatherapy and almond milk lattes, I have bad news. The mattress is lumpy, your roommate snores like a wounded walrus, and the beverage cart is a choice between weak coffee and tap water. But you are alive to complain about it. And that, surprisingly, is the point.

You did not come here for a vacation. You came here because your life caught fire. And now, for the first time in a long time, someone is telling you to stop, drop, and sit down long enough to learn how not to burn again.

The introduction to this place is always the same. You walk through those double doors clutching whatever is left of your dignity and immediately think, *"Wait a minute, I am paying for this?"* The first thing they hand you is a urine cup, and the second thing they do is take your phone. No valet. No welcome drink. No spa robe. Just a tech named *Trevor* who has seen too much and says, *"You will get used to it,"* with the weary confidence of a man who has lived through six apocalypses and one staff potluck. There is no room service here. The only thing getting turned down is your excuses.

And yet, every rehab has that one guy walking around like he booked his stay through *Expedia*. He is on day two, wearing flip-flops, whispering, *"Do you have soy milk?"* Sir, you were drinking hand sanitizer behind a *Circle K* last week. This is not the moment for dairy preferences.

By lunchtime, you have met your new family, the most dysfunctional, lovable cast of humans you never knew you needed. A week ago, you would have crossed the street to avoid these people, and now you are comparing snack stashes and trauma.

There is *Big Country*, your roommate. He is six-foot-five, smells like menthol and bad decisions, and sleeps with a CPAP machine that sounds like *Darth Vader* gargling soup. Every night you lie there thinking, *"How did I go from bar crawls to bedtime stories with this man?"*

Then there is *Ashley*. She has eleven ex-husbands, six kinds of nicotine, and eyeliner on at seven in the morning. She has been here three times and swears she is nailing it this round. She is miserable, but she will still offer you her last ginger ale and half of her nicotine patch like it is a sacred ritual.

And then there is *Spider.* *Spider* is the most emotionally intelligent man you will ever meet, even though he has a neck tattoo that says FRITOS for reasons no one has ever been brave enough to ask. We respect the art. He has been through overdoses, prison, heartbreak, and more second chances than the DMV gives out, and somehow he arrived here wiser than anyone with a GED has a right to be.

Just when you think the cast is complete, you meet the staff, the real supporting characters who keep this circus upright while everyone else is emotionally falling down the stairs. The techs are like older cousins at a family reunion who have seen things. They have been sober anywhere from six months to six minutes, and they love saying, "*I have seen worse,*" which is never comforting. They are equal parts babysitter, therapist, security guard, crisis negotiator, and the human embodiment of "*I cannot believe I am not getting paid more for this.*" They will burst into your room at six in the morning with a blood pressure cuff and do room checks at three in the morning with flashlights like they are hunting raccoons in the attic.

The nurses here are built different. You could run up to the nurses' station foaming at the mouth and yelling, "*Jesus told me to eat the drywall,*" and they would blink twice, hand you a cup of water, and say, "*Okay hon, but you are late for group. Let's go.*" At this point, you could sprout wings and start speaking fluent dolphin, and they would calmly reply, "*You can talk to your counselor about that.*"

And speaking of counselors, they are therapy gangsters. They seem so normal until they open their mouths, and suddenly

3

they are emotional snipers. You mention your DUI like it is a traffic ticket, and they hit you with, *"And how did that make you feel?"* and your entire personality collapses. Next thing you know, you are crying about the *Easy-Bake Oven* you did not get in 1983 and the fact your mother never hugged you after your third-grade choir recital.

One day you are out there running the streets, and the next you are begging a nurse for *Imodium* and being told you cannot wear your hoodie in group. And somehow it works. You want to run. Everyone does. But if you stay, if you sit still long enough to feel your feelings instead of drowning them, something starts to shift. Not suddenly. More like thawing.

Because this place is not where people come to die. It is where they come to stop dying. It is where people crawl out of graves every single day and remember how to laugh again. And that is better than room service. That is redemption.

Rehab is not a resort. It is a factory reset for human beings. No filters. No substances. Just you, your guilt, and a counselor named *Lewis* trying to explain Step Four with a dry-erase marker that ran out in 2016. But it works, slowly and beautifully. You remember what it feels like to wake up sober, safe, and maybe even grateful. This place breaks you open, but that is the only way light gets in.

So stop looking for mints on your pillow and start thanking the universe for a pillow at all. You did not come here for comfort. You came here for courage. And courage never comes with room service. You can spend your time counting what is wrong with this place, or you can start counting what is right. You can blame the coffee, the mattress, your counselor, or the moon, or you can look in the mirror and finally say, "*Alright, partner. We have run out of excuses.*"

Because this is not about comfort. It is about waking up. The comfort zone is where dreams die, and if you are uncomfortable right now, congratulations. You are exactly where you are supposed to be.

And this squeaky bed, bleach-smelling, emotionally over-crowded rehab is the first safe place you have had in years. You will sit in group drinking mop water coffee, listening to *Spider* talk about robbing a *Taco Bell* with a spoon, and you will laugh so hard you almost spill it. You will pass *Ashley* a cigarette, and she will hand you a warm *Werther's Original* that has been in her pocket way too long. You will hear *Big Country* praying softly at night that his son sees him as a hero again someday, and something inside you stirs. Hope, maybe. Or peace.

And when it hits you that you almost missed this, this chaos, this grace, this chance, you finally understand why lowering your *Yelp* standards here is the first step to raising your life standards out there. Because it is rehab, not the *Ritz*, not a spa, not a resort with towel animals and cucumber water. It is the place you came when you decided you were done dying and ready to live.

And this time, you are checking out with your soul.

10 Signs You're Not at the Hotel *(and that's a good thing!):*

1- The mint on your pillow is actually a cough drop the last patient left behind.

2- Turn-down service means your roommate accidentally knocked your blanket onto the floor.

3- The *"spa treatment"* is a five-minute hot shower before the water turns arctic in shower shoes.

4- Your view is either the parking lot, the dumpster, or a guy aggressively power-walking in circles- like if he stops moving he might actually feel feelings.

5- Room service is you, walking to the cafeteria before the bacon is gone.

6- The wake-up call is your counselor banging on the door yelling, *"Group in five!"*

7- Housekeeping will not be leaving you towel animals on your bed. If your towel suspiciously resembles a swan, it's because *Big Country* used it as a napkin.

8- The *"pillow menu"* is one flat one or one lumpy one... choose wisely.

9- Evening entertainment is someone in the lounge telling the exact same story they told yesterday but with hand gestures. Intense.

10- The *"continental breakfast"* is one bruised banana, some off-brand cereal, and a guy named *Kyle* telling you his whole life story before 8 a.m.- Then the tech *Trevor* walks by and asks, *"You need anything?"* Yes *Trevor*. I need boundaries. And nicotine.

2

The Gift Of Pause (The Closest Thing To A "Life Timeout" You'll Ever Get)

At first, rehab feels like punishment. The rules, the schedule, the fact that someone else decides when you eat lunch, none of it screams tropical retreat. But then one day, if you are lucky, it hits you. This is not hell. This is the pause you never gave yourself. This is the moment life finally slammed the brakes before you drove yourself off the cliff. This is a gift disguised as inconvenience.

When in your entire adult life has anyone ever said to you, *"You do not have to work right now. You do not have to hustle. You do not have to fix anyone's mess or outrun your own. All you have to do is stay alive and start again."* That is what rehab really is. Not punishment. Not prison. A timeout from chaos, a second chance disguised as structure, the one place where you are allowed to sit down and take the first real breath you have taken in years.

It is the only place on Earth where people will cheer like you won the *Super Bowl* just because you remembered it is your laundry day. Except this time, the trophy is not a ring. It is your life back. You are surrounded by an entire staff whose only job is to help you not set yourself on fire every week. It is rehab softly saying, *"Here, sit down. Catch your breath. Let's figure out how to live without breaking yourself in the process."*

Sure, the walls are beige enough to make oatmeal look glamorous, the furniture looks like it was rescued from a church basement, and your roommate's shoes smell like they have been through something traumatic. But beneath all that ugliness, something beautiful happens. The noise fades. The chaos dulls. You realize you do not have to keep running. Not today. Not right now. You get to rest, and real rest feels foreign at first, almost suspicious, because you have spent so long living in survival mode that peace feels like a trick.

But in that pause, healing creeps in. Quietly. Gently. You start to hear your own thoughts again, not the panicked ones, not the shame-soaked ones, but the real ones. You start remembering pieces of yourself you thought were gone. You stop seeing yourself as the person who broke everything and start seeing the person who is strong enough to rebuild.

Stillness does not mean weakness. Stillness means you finally stopped running long enough for your soul to catch up.

Rehab is the hallway between who you were and who you are

9

becoming, that sacred, uncomfortable middle place where nothing is fully repaired yet, but nothing is fully wrecked anymore. Sometimes the greatest gift you can receive is not another chance at life. It is the chance to pause long enough to believe one is possible.

Because in the chaos of the world, nobody gets a pause button. Nobody gets a moment to stop, breathe, and reset. Unless they are lucky enough to land somewhere that hands them one and says, "*Here. Use it.*"

7 Things You Don't Have to Deal With in Rehab:

1- Unspoken prayer requests on *Facebook* (*Like girl... what is it? Gallstones? Divorce? Pyramid scheme? You're not about to trick me into DMing you just so you can sell me essential oils*)

2- Office small talk about "*what you did this weekend.*" (*Nobody actually cares, Cheryl*)

3- Dodging debt collectors: They can call all they want — you're basically in witness protection.

4- You don't have to pretend you like *Janet's "famous"* potato salad at the family reunion.

5- Grocery store lines where the person ahead of you is having a speakerphone conversation. ("*No Brenda I didn't want to know your cat has IBS. Neither did the other 12 strangers now invested.")*

6– You don't have to explain to your mom for the 87th time how to attach a file to an email like you're a professor at *MIT*.

7– You don't have to hear "*let's circle back*" in a meeting that could have been an email.

3

Detox: The Flu You Paid For

Welcome to detox. Not in the "*yay, confetti*" way, but in the "*you didn't die and somehow landed here*" way. That counts as a win, even if you currently feel like reheated garbage. Your brain is screaming for substances, your body has staged a full-blown coup, and someone just handed you a plastic cup of pills with names that sound like rejected *Scrabble* words. The lights are fluorescent, the thermostat is apparently set for penguins, and time is doing something deeply suspicious. You swear you have been here fourteen hours, but the clock insists it has been twenty-two minutes.

Detox always starts the same way: with the absolute certainty that you are dying. Not metaphorically or poetically. Theatrically. You will make a whole will out loud. Tell my kids I love them. Bury me with my vape. But by Day Three, you realize something shocking. You are not dying at all. You are just alive for the first time in years, and your body has some notes. They hand you *Tylenol* and *Gatorade* like it is holy water, and you drink it because you are desperate. But let's be real. If *Gatorade* could fix what is wrong with you, you would have been healed at a gas station in 2014. Meanwhile, your body is offended, confused, and filing HR complaints against you in real time. Every single sound becomes disrespectful. The air conditioner is too loud. Your roommate's breathing is rude. Your own heartbeat is aggressive. You are sweating through your sheets like they insulted your ancestors. You hallucinate that your blanket called you a quitter. Everything hurts. Everything is loud. Everything is wrong.

Detox is like paying nine hundred dollars a night to get jumped by your own bloodstream. It is the flu with a cover charge. You are not sipping cucumber water. You are sipping regret. Your body starts collecting every bad decision since 2004 and cashing them in all at once. You sweat out sin, shame, sodium, and whatever emotional debris you have been hoarding. Every muscle you forgot existed starts screaming, *"actually, we have some things to say."* And then you look around the unit and realize you are not alone in your personal apocalypse. The place looks like a shelter for feral emotions. Someone is praying to *Jesus, Buddha*, and sometimes *7-Eleven*. One guy keeps yelling, *"my skin itches." Spider*, calm as a monk, says, *"that is just guilt leaving the body,"* with such confidence you actually scratch to test the theory. Someone else is asking every hour, *"y'all got any biscuits?"* In another room, a man curls up clutching a crumpled photo of his son and cries so quietly it breaks the air. You stop seeing strangers and start seeing wrecked humans becoming real again.

The staff has the energy of a *Waffle House* waitress at three in the morning. Serene. Unbothered. Emotionally fireproof. You are over here bargaining over graham crackers, and they stroll in saying, *"vitals time."* They give you *Ibuprofen* like it is morphine. They hand you a toddler-sized plastic cup of tap water like it is liquid salvation. They say, *"you are doing great._"* Ma'am, I just hallucinated my childhood hamster singing *Freebird*. I do not think I am doing great. But their calm is contagious. If they are not panicking, maybe you do not have to either.

Detox is not just your body freaking out. Your emotions wake up too. Every regret you buried comes pounding on the door like debt collectors. Loud. Unapologetic. Not taking no for an answer. One moment you are swearing off substances forever. The next you are praying for death or ginger ale, whichever arrives first. The worst moment is not the sweating or shaking. It is the quiet thought that whispers, *"you could make this stop."* And for the first time in a long time, you whisper back, *"yeah, but I will not."* That whisper is the first honest promise you have made to yourself in ages.

Then slowly, something shifts. Your hands shake less. You sleep an hour. You laugh, really laugh, and it does not feel fake. Sunlight looks like sunlight instead of a threat. It is not dramatic. It is a flicker. A breath. But in detox, a flicker is everything. It is your body whispering, *"I never hated you. I just needed you to stop poisoning me so I could fight for you again."*

Detox is sweatpants, bad coffee, and ceiling tiles you count like they owe you money. It is your body throwing a tantrum while your soul quietly rebuilds itself. But it is also the doorway. The first real step. If you can survive these few days without bolting for the exit, you might surprise yourself. Because in a place where the bar for joy is a *Sprite*, a blanket, and a moment of stillness, you are doing something miraculous. You are waking up without needing to escape yourself. And that is the beginning of freedom.

10 Ways You Know You're in Detox:

1- The techs don't knock — they bust into your room like the *Kool-Aid Man* with a blood pressure cuff.

2- The every-30-minute flashlight checks aren't about count-ing respirations — they're about slowly breaking your will.

3- Every TV is permanently stuck on *Judge Judy* or the *Weather Channel*, and no one questions it.

4- The mattress feels like it was made of plywood and bad decisions.

5- Shower shoes aren't optional — they're survival gear.

6- Every doctor has a built-in BS detector — and you still try anyway.

7- Somebody is smuggling contraband snacks into their room like they're the *Pablo Escobar* of *Lay's*.

8- You instinctively reach for your phone to *Google "how to address an envelope"...* then remember it's in a lockbox.

9- Someone yells "*Meds!*" and the line forms faster than *Black Friday* at *Best Buy*.

10- Rec therapy makes you feel like you're seven again: "*We get to go outside?! For real?!*"

4

Can I Actually Do This?

At some point in those first few days, you are going to ask yourself the big question: Can I actually do this? And by "*this*," you mean stay in rehab, sit with your feelings, not bolt at the first sign of discomfort, and somehow exist without your old escape hatch. You will ask it in the shower. You will ask it while staring out the window like you are trapped in a *Sarah McLachlan ASPCA* commercial, silently begging the universe to either rescue you, adopt you, or at least send someone to bail you out for less than the cost of a cup of coffee a day. You will ask it lying on your pillow wondering how much easier it would be to simply just... *not*.

You sit on your bed with your belongings stuffed into a flimsy plastic bag like you have just been evicted from your own existence. You stare at the wall like it owes you back rent. That is when it slips out, so quietly you barely hear yourself say it.

"*I can't do this.*" And the wild part is that might be the first truly honest thing you have said to yourself in years. Recovery does not begin when you feel brave. It begins when you feel like a fragile, confused creature who wants to run, and you still show up again the next day anyway.

The first few days feel like your brain is trying to climb out through your eyebrows. Everyone in group is crying about things you did not even know could be sad. The kid next to you is confessing something involving a lost ferret and a trampoline mishap, and you are staring at your knees thinking, "*Please God, someone in this room better have answers.*" You are exhausted. You have not slept right. Your stomach is confused. You are almost certain someone stole your socks even though you absolutely did not pack any.

I remember my second day in rehab so clearly it still lives in my nervous system. I had already decided I was done. I was packing my belongings in that plastic bag loudly and dramatically, like I wanted the entire unit to witness my exit. I marched into the hallway with the determination of someone who had no ride, no plan, no money, and no idea where the parking lot even was.

They sent a young counselor to stop me. She looked about twelve and held a clipboard she definitely did not need. She had the soft, overly calm voice of someone who has only experienced conflict while returning something at *Target*. She stood there with perfect posture and said, in her most professional tone, "*Okay, but before you go, let's explore what leaving represents to you emotionally.*" Ma'am. It represents me leaving.

I opened my mouth to start my dramatic speech, but before I could begin, a housekeeper rolled up beside me. No clipboard. No jargon. Just a woman who had seen more breakdowns than the nurses and more arguments than the counselors. She placed her hand on my shoulder, looked me straight in the face, and said, "*You don't have to want to stay. You only have to not leave.*"

And for reasons I still cannot fully explain, that sentence landed. Not the clinical language. Not the therapeutic tone. Not the fancy treatment plan. Her. The woman pushing a cart of clean towels said the one sentence that kept me there.

That was the moment I realized recovery is not about being strong. It is about being honest. It is about admitting when you are scared and letting someone walk you back from the edge. It is learning that failure is not final. It is often just a sign that you need to keep going in a different direction.

Nobody arrives in treatment ready. Nobody walks in brave. We show up cracked open, terrified, hopeful, and exhausted all at the same time. And that is not a flaw. That is the doorway.

Recovery is not one big decision. It is a thousand small ones. You just need to be willing. Willing to show up. Willing to be seen. Willing to let someone else believe in you until you have enough strength to believe in yourself again. Willing to take the first small steps toward a life you do not hate. Not the old way, not anymore. This is the new way, *a willing way.*

And if you stay long enough, if you breathe through the urge to run, if you get through the fog and the doubt and the fear, something strange starts to happen. Somewhere between the cravings and the crying, you catch yourself staring at *Spider's* tattoo like it is an encrypted message from the streets, wondering what felonies a man has to commit to earn *FRITOS* as ink. You sit there thinking, "*Something went down at that 7-Eleven, and I will not heal until I have answers.*"

And while you are still trying to decode that mystery, something inside you eventually blinks awake. It does not shout. It does not perform. It simply whispers with a quiet, steady truth, "*I think I might actually be able to do this.*"

Not forever. Not perfectly. But today.

And in recovery, *today* is how you build a life.

8 Signs That You Can Do Rehab:

1- If you can get *Narcaned* in the *Wendy's* parking lot at 1 AM and still wake up craving a *Frosty* — you can do rehab.

2- If you've pawned your grandma's DVD player twice and she still lets you in the house — you can do rehab.

3- If you've ever used your own shoelace as medical equipment — you can do rehab.

4- If your bilirubin is so high, strangers keep complimenting your *"golden glow"* — you can do rehab.

5- If you've ever taken apart three radios, a blender, and a toaster *"for parts"* and built absolutely nothing — you can do rehab.

6- If you've done the addict calculus of *"if I take three tonight, that's two tomorrow, plus maybe I can borrow one"* — you can do rehab.

7- If you've ever told your kid *"we'll go tomorrow"* knowing damn well you weren't — you can do rehab.

8- If you've opened an *Amazon* package you ordered in a blackout and said, *"What the actual f*** is this?"* — you can do rehab.

5

The Staff—Your New Temporary Family (Whether You Like It Or Not)

The staff in treatment are a special breed. Half of them are in recovery. The other half are one group session away from needing to be. They have smelled everything, heard everything, and seen things that cannot be unseen without prayer and bleach. They are not your regular humans. They work twelve-hour shifts with twelve cents in their checking accounts while managing forty grown adults who behave like toddlers at summer camp.

"Don't go in that room." "Put your shoes on." "No touching. I mean it."

Sometimes they work actual magic because there is no other explanation for how they appear out of thin air the moment you try to sneak an extra snack from another unit. You cannot shock them. You could walk in completely naked saying, *"The aliens told me to detox,"* and they would hand you a towel and say, *"We will talk about that in group."* Their days are basically holding one person's hand and saying, *"You have got this,"* while simultaneously yelling across the hall, *"Put the fire extinguisher down, Travis!"*

At first, you swear they are out to ruin your life. They say no a lot. No, you cannot skip group. No, you cannot have your phone. No, you cannot leave just because you feel better now. But let's be honest. If you had this much structure and consistency earlier in life, you might not have needed rehab in the first place. They do not let you manipulate. They do not let you pout for twenty-four hours straight. They are not afraid to tell you that you are being ridiculous.

And while you might not appreciate them in the moment, especially when they wake you up for morning vitals like they are personally offended that you are asleep, trust me, you will miss them when you leave. You will realize they were not trying to keep you prisoner. They were trying to keep you alive.

After a while, the staff stop feeling like authority figures and start feeling like characters in your own weird rehab sitcom. There is the perky one who bounces into 9 a.m. meditation like she microdosed sunshine for breakfast. She claps her hands and says things like *"Today is a fresh start"* and *"Good vibes only,"* while thirty sleep-deprived addicts mentally try to set her aura on fire and hiss at her like dehydrated cats.

Then there is the stoic one. He moves slowly and intentionally,

23

like somebody who once lost a fistfight to a goose and never emotionally recovered. He has the emotional range of a tax auditor. He speaks three times a day, tops, and somehow he is everyone's favorite.

And finally, the scary one. She is the staff member who looks like she has escorted demons out of group therapy using only her tone of voice. You swear she teleports. You blink, and she is suddenly behind you asking, "*Where are you supposed to be?*" She would definitely unplug your life support to charge her vape and then ask, "*You good?*" Somehow, she is the only person you trust when everything goes to hell.

By the time you leave, you look at their rules with quiet respect. You finally understand why they checked your pockets, why they cut off your four-hour rants, and why they would not let you make phone calls while you were still vibrating with emotion. They were not following protocol. They were protecting you from yourself.

They annoy you. They call you out. They make you cry with their tough love. But they also hold your secrets without flinching. They sit with your pain without looking away. They see your potential long before you do. And it hits you one day, out of nowhere, while you are watching the tech yell at *Travis* again, while a nurse carrying a metal tray of tiny paper cups passes out meds like holy communion, and while you are sitting in group wondering why every counselor looks like they either used to be in a rock band or escaped a cult with merch still on. These people were never just staff. They were the family you did not know you needed.

They are the ones who saw you at your absolute worst and treated you like there was something worth saving. So no, they are not your concierge. They will not fluff your pillow or bring you a menu. But they will help you stay alive, stay sober, and maybe, just maybe, start believing you are worth the work. Because in rehab, the staff might not give you what you want. But they will fight like hell to give you what you need.

10 Rehab Staff Archetypes:

1- The Snack Police
Finds your hidden Doritos stash like they've got a K9 nose for contraband. You're left with nothing but shame and a half-eaten granola bar.

2- The Lighter Gatekeeper
Holds the community lighter like it's the Holy Grail. Makes you feel like you're signing a lease just to get a spark.

3- The Doctor: The Human Exit Sign
Keeps their hand on the doorknob the entire visit. You're basically yelling your symptoms down the hallway as they walk away.

4- The Seen-It-All Nurse
You ask for meds because you're anxious, they say, "*We don't medicate feelings.*" And that, my friend, IS REHAB IN A NUTSHELL.

5- The *"So What I Hear You Saying"* Counselor

Asks, *"Where've you been?"* and you say, *"The bathroom."*
Then they repeat it back — *"So what I hear you saying is... you
were in the bathroom?"* — and suddenly you're questioning
what the hell you were actually doing in there.

6- The Group Gatekeeper

Shuts the door right as you walk up, like you're late for a
flight. Now you're stuck staring through the window while
everyone inside pretends not to make eye contact.

7- The Call-You-Out Counselor

Has no problem putting you on blast in front of the whole
group. You thought you were flying under the radar, but nope
— welcome to center stage.

8- The Cool-Parent Staff

Looks the other way and lets you stay up past lights out. In
that moment, they're not staff — they're your best friend with
the keys to the kingdom.

9- The Reliable Med Nurse

You see them on shift and already feel calmer. This isn't the
day you'll be told, *"We don't medicate feelings."*

10- The Schedule-Check Staff

They're so chill you actually ask when they're working next.
Not because you care about their life — but because rehab sucks
less when they're around.

6

Missing Home (Even If Home Was A Dumpster Fire)

.

At some point in rehab, a wave of homesickness will slam into you out of nowhere. Maybe it is a smell, a song, or just a painfully average Tuesday where absolutely nothing is happening. Suddenly you are daydreaming about your bed, your shower, your coffee mug, your couch... all the comforts you swore you hated before you got here.

Sometimes the home you miss is the same home you could not stand living in. The one where you were lonely or miserable or neck-deep in chaos. Your brain becomes a liar, man. It is like one of those dudes who only remembers his ex's eyelashes and not the fact that she keyed his *Camry*. It edits the footage. You do not remember the fighting, the bills, the hiding, the way you lived in survival mode. You remember the *"nice"* parts: your favorite blanket, your dog's tail wag, the exact hum of your refrigerator at two in the morning. Suddenly the depressing one-bedroom apartment where you cried into questionable lunch meat becomes a cozy sanctuary with excellent acoustics and a charcuterie board that looks like *Gordon Ramsay* plated it himself.

Missing home does not mean you made a mistake coming here. It means you are human. Even unhealthy routines gave you a sense of control. In rehab, everything is brand new — your bed, your schedule, your food, your neighbors. You are sharing a toilet with strangers and your free time is monitored like you are back in middle school detention. Of course you miss familiarity. Nothing screams comfort like being able to fart in peace.

The danger is romanticizing the past. Homesickness can twist into, *"Maybe it was not that bad,"* and that is the same slippery thinking that leads people right back into relapse. The truth is, the *"home"* you think you miss right now is a highlight reel, not the full documentary.

The trick is separating *"home"* the place from *"home"* the feeling. You can get the feeling back: comfort, safety, belonging. You just have to build it somewhere new with healthier habits and surroundings. You do not have to return to the old address to feel at home again.

Until then, you can create small pockets of home right where you are. Maybe it is making your bed the way you always did. Maybe it is writing a nightly letter to someone you trust. Maybe it is a playlist of songs you love that do not send you spiraling. These tiny comforts keep you grounded while you are rebuilding. They remind you that home is not four walls and a couch with questionable stains. Home is the feeling of belonging, of safety, of slowly stitching your life back together.

And the best part? This time, you get to choose what home looks like. No more dumpster fires disguised as cozy nostalgia. This one is built with intention, not survival.

Missing home is not weakness. It is a reminder of what matters. The goal is not just to go back. It is to return as someone healthier, steadier, and finally at home in your own skin.

8 Signs You're Missing Home:

1- You daydream about scrolling your phone on the toilet for 45 minutes without anyone judging you for it.

2- You miss falling asleep to *Netflix* asking, *"Are you still watching?"* — like it was the only one who truly cared.

3- You miss the days when you didn't know the 7-day forecast by heart, plus the *Doppler* radar pattern — information you never once wanted, needed, or asked for.

4- You stare at the snack bar and think, *They don't have my chips.* Suddenly you're ready to walk out over the lack of *Cool*

Ranch Doritos.

5- You miss your couch, even though one cushion smells like vomit and the other like a wet dog and regret.

6- You miss the smell of your shampoo — even if it was *Suave 3-in-1* that doubled as car wash soap.

7- You miss your wife saying, *"Do whatever you want,"* knowing full well it was a trap.

8- You miss your kids ignoring you until the *Wi-Fi* goes out and suddenly they actually speak to you.

7

Strangers Who Become Your People

You walk into rehab certain you are alone. You believe your shame is unique and your pain too personal to share. You think your story is the worst one in the room. And then, one by one, the strangers begin to speak. The people you meet in rehab are not like the people you meet anywhere else on Earth. This is not brunch or the PTA or "*Hi, I am Janice, I love my husband and we are redoing our kitchen in quartz.*" No. This is, "*Hi, I am Angie. I once drove drunk with my toddler in the car to get more beer; I have not washed my crotch in four days, and if my husband gets hit by a falling tree today, that would be fine by me.*" And somehow, you love *Angie* instantly. Because she told the truth. *Janice* never did. Outside of rehab, friendship is curated. You bond over shared tastes and hobbies and carefully filtered versions of yourself. In rehab, you bond over survival. It is trauma *Tinder*. "*You got abandonment issues and a nicotine patch? Swipe right, sister.*" There is something holy about the way you can speak loud and messy and wrong and still get a hug instead of a gasp. You realize people do not just see your worst. They understand it. You look at each other and think, "*You too? Damn.*" That is not shame. That is freedom.

People who came in ready to fight, lie, or shut down start laughing, crying, and protecting each other like they had known one another since kindergarten. Rehab turns strangers into family faster than Thanksgiving turns family into enemies. Before recovery, I did not have real friends. Not the kind who checked on me or stayed when things got hard. I pushed everyone away. My world shrank until it was me, my addiction, and a silence that gnawed through my ribs. Isolation felt safer, so when I got to treatment, my plan was simple: keep to myself, head down, do my time, do not get attached. That plan lasted maybe thirty-six hours. Because rehab cracks you open whether you like it or not. You sit in group and someone says something you have thought for years but never admitted out loud. Suddenly it feels like they broke into your mind and stole a page from your diary.

The people in rehab are characters. Forget *Tiger King*. Forget whatever show *Netflix* is pushing this week. These are the real characters. These people did not care about my résumé, my past, or the mask I had worn for years. They saw me messy, crying in pajamas, pacing hallways at three in the morning, saying things I swore I would take to the grave. And instead of backing away, they leaned in. It is disorienting at first, being around people who do not want anything from you except honesty. Trust builds fast here, because when you are both crawling out of the same pit, you do not waste time pretending you are not covered in mud. We laughed at jokes only rehab people understand. We whispered during quiet hours and got in trouble for absolutely nothing. We shared snacks and cigarettes and ramen hacks and war stories that would make outsiders clutch their pearls, while in here everyone nodded and said, *"That's nothing, man."*

Not everyone becomes your best friend. Some people get on your nerves. Some test your patience. Some push boundaries like it is their *Olympic* sport. But even those people teach you something. Healing means learning to live alongside all kinds of humans without combusting. And then come the goodbyes. Oh my, the goodbyes. Standing in the lobby hugging someone you have only known three weeks, crying like you're sending your child off to war. It is ridiculous. It is beautiful. It wrecks you. These are the people who saw you at your worst and did not flinch, the ones who clapped when you got your chip even though their own hands were shaking, the ones who told you the truth you did not want to hear. You did not just get clean. You got found.

What you share in rehab cannot be unshared. It becomes its own language, its own bond, its own proof that connection is still possible after everything tried to convince you otherwise. Years from now, your husband will be ranting about his truck's *Bluetooth* refusing to connect and how *Costco* betrayed your family by discontinuing your size of trash bags. You will nod politely while your brain, exhausted by the mundane, finds its way back to the only place life ever felt completely honest and unexpectedly full of purpose. You will remember *Amphibian Abby*, the nineteen-year-old who found a baby turtle during smoke break and immediately declared it her emotional support child. She carried that thing in her hoodie pocket everywhere she went. Group therapy. Med line. Meal line. That turtle saw more healing than most licensed counselors. Technically it was against the rules. Technically it was unhygienic. Technically the turtle smelled like a gator's armpit going through menopause, a divorce, and a midlife career change. Technically she was probably spreading *Salmonella*. But nobody said a word. Because deep down, everyone understood what it felt like to hold onto something small and helpless because you did not know how to hold yourself yet. They let her have that turtle. They let her keep that tiny, swamp-scented piece of comfort. They let her love something even when she did not feel lovable. And when staff finally convinced her to set him free in the courtyard pond, the entire unit gathered like it was a royal funeral. She cried. We cried. Even the scary staff member wiped a tear she pretended she did not have. It was messy and weird and gentle and borderline illegal, but it was real.

You will remember *Guard Dog Gary*, who formed a full *Neighborhood Watch* inside the facility like we were living in a gated community instead of a busted rehab. He made pamphlets on notebook paper and held official meetings every Sunday at four o'clock sharp. Everybody showed up, not because we believed danger was lurking in the rec room, but because we all knew it gave him purpose. Even the night shift tech let him borrow an extra flashlight. Looking back, it was never the pamphlets or the patrols that mattered. It was the way we circled around one lonely man and said, without saying it, "we *see you, you matter, show us what you have*." That is friendship in rehab, loving people in the exact weird shape they come in.

You will remember *Mailbox Marvin*, the sixty-eight-year-old veteran who did not have anybody on the outside writing him letters, so the whole unit stepped in. Five different people wrote to him every day using fake names and stamps and even little doodles so he would feel special when the mail cart came around. He thought he was the most popular man in rehab. *"Got another one from Doris,"* he would say proudly, holding up the envelope like he had won the lottery. *Doris* was actually *Rodney* from Room Twelve who could not spell Wednesday. *Marvin* would sit on his bed reading each one like it was scripture. *"Look here,"* he would say, *"my cousin Earl says he is praying for me."* *Earl* was *Vanessa*, who did not even believe in prayer but committed to the bit so hard she wrote him a sermon and a recipe for cornbread. Everyone used different handwriting, different tone, different stories, just to make sure *Marvin* never felt alone. Anywhere else, this would be identity theft and felony mail fraud. In rehab, it was community service.

These people were not your blood, but somehow they showed you a deeper kind of care. The kind where everyone instinctively knows who needs softness, who needs belonging, and who needs purpose. You can keep *Janice* and her quartz countertops. I will take *Angie*. The broken. The honest. The halfway-healed. The funny. Those are my people. The ones who came back from the edge and decided to try again. Out here in the real world, everyone goes back to pretending. In rehab, your mess was your membership card. You belonged there, not in spite of your brokenness, but because of it. It was the first place your wounds did not disqualify you. They introduced you.

So when you finally walk out that door with your discharge papers, and *Marvin* shuffles up and hands you a letter addressed to *Doris*, who does not exist, and whispers, *"Make sure she gets this,"* and Angie hollers across the lobby, *"Text me if you do not die, bit**,"* you start laughing and crying at the same time. Because somehow, these absolute weirdos became your people. And once you have loved people at their messiest, the shame you carried your whole life finally starts to loosen its grip. Those people loved me at a time when I could not even stand myself, and they did not know a single thing about me beyond the pain I walked in with. Not even my last name. That is the kind of unconditional acceptance that rewires a human being. You realize maybe you were not the villain. Maybe you were human and hurting and doing the best you could with pain nobody ever taught you to carry. And somehow, walking out with that truth feels like the start of everything.

10 Signs You Actually Found Real Friends in Rehab:

1- They warn you not to overshare in group by kicking your chair under the table — subtle enough staff can't prove it.

2- You know the exact pitch of their *"staff's coming"* cough and trust it more than an alarm system.

3- You've already schemed out which sober living you're both applying to, like it's college dorm assignments.

4- You create roast names together for everyone else in treatment that you'll never forget —*like "Xanax Betty."*

5- They saved you a seat in the TV room — that's basically them handing you a shank in prison and saying, *"I got you."*

6- They clapped when you finally admitted your "*drug dealer*" was just your cousin *Chad*.

7- You both got scolded for laughing during someone's tragic story... and staff gave you *"the look,"* which only made it funnier, because nothing bonds people like being terrible humans together.

8- They help you hide extra sugar packets in your Bible because *"no one checks Leviticus."*

9- They were the first to roast you when your AMA threat failed because your mom wouldn't pick you up.

10- They'll call you out mid-share: *"Girl, quit lying — you were drunk, but not that drunk."*

8

Group Time (Where Therapy Meets Reality TV Without The Cameras)

The first time you walk into group, it looks like absolute chaos. It is a circle of mismatched chairs, fluorescent lighting, and faces that look like they have survived twelve seasons of a show nobody would ever volunteer to watch. For a split second, you cannot tell if we are about to do therapy, play *Duck Duck Goose*, or be inducted into our first *séance*. Nobody knows the rules. Nobody knows who is sharing next. Half the room looks like they are waiting on lab results. Someone is crying, someone is detoxing, and one guy is asleep with his eyes open like a lizard. And you sit there thinking, how in the world did all of us end up in the same room?

You do not mean to relate, but you do. You do not mean to care, but you do. You do not mean to cry, but suddenly it is happening anyway. Group is wild like that. You are in a room full of people who drove their lives into ditches, some metaphorical and some very literal, and somehow you start building a community out of the wreckage. There is always that moment when the counselor cheerfully asks who wants to start, and instantly twelve grown adults become fascinated by invisible lint on their pants. Everybody studies the floor tiles like they are suddenly the most interesting thing they have ever seen. Someone raises a hand just to ask if they can use the restroom, even though we all received the lecture about going before group.

Then someone finally shares. Maybe it is small. Maybe it is heartbreak. Maybe it is funny. Maybe it is tragic. But somebody says something true, something with loss or guilt or fear or shame or hope tucked inside it, and suddenly heads begin to nod because we all know that feeling. Addiction steals connection. It takes your routine, your structure, your community, and your belief that your voice matters. Group gives it back, one story at a time.

Sometimes group feels like church. Sometimes it feels like a courtroom. Sometimes it has the energy of a family reunion where you are pretty sure someone is about to start a fight in the parking lot. Sometimes it feels like a comedy club where you laugh so hard you forget why you were sad in the first place. And sometimes it is straight-up ridiculous. There is always that one person who starts with, "*I do not usually talk,*" and then proceeds to talk for forty-seven minutes straight, covering childhood, all three divorces, a possum named *Greg*, two unpaid traffic tickets, and the night they were banned from *Chili's* corporate-wide. There is the spiritual one who says things like, *"Life is like a river, you know?"* Sir, no, it is not. You were bathing with a wet wipe in a *Love's* truck stop bathroom. Let's stay present. Then there is the person who says they relapsed because their roommate breathed too hard. No, buddy. You relapsed because you relapsed. Let's own it. There is always *Miss "I am not sharing but I am judging,"* who sits staring at everyone like she is *IRS*-auditing their trauma. And then there is *Spider*. He speaks in riddles that sound like parables but are actually crimes. When someone new asks about his tattoo, he mutters, *"Man, I am not proud of what I had to do,"* and the room goes silent because nobody knows what he means and nobody wants to ask.

Even with all the absurdity, group somehow becomes the first place you have ever been allowed to speak without interruption. The first place someone listens without judging. The first place you are told the truth instead of a soft lie. You learn quickly that people do not get better by being coddled. They get better by being challenged. When someone calls you out in group, it is not an attack. It is a gift. It means they believe you are capable of more than the bare-minimum scraps you have been surviving on. In group, your worst day is someone else's *"Yeah, Tuesday."*

There is a quiet magic that happens when someone finally shares something they have carried alone for years and the room does not flinch. Nobody gasps. Nobody gets up to leave. People simply nod, like they have been waiting on you. I have watched people who thought they had nothing in common hear one familiar sentence and feel something inside them unlock. Addiction is an equalizer, and so is hope. Group is where we practice belonging before we believe we deserve it.

By week two, you are attached. You notice who sits where. You get protective. You think, why are you in *Spider's* seat? He always sits there. When someone leaves, whether they graduate or relapse, the circle feels wrong. A beat off. A little emptier. Because you learned their voice, their fight, their laugh that cracked the tension, their story that mirrored a piece of your own. By the end of group, you are emotionally dehydrated, spiritually exfoliated, and somehow lighter. You have laughed, cried, confessed something borderline illegal, and connected with people who now know you better than your own family.

It is messy. It is chaotic. It is sacred. It is healing. It is group.

8 Unspoken Rules of Group Time:

1- After roll call, *Bathroom Brad* always disappears for 33 minutes like he's running a secret *Etsy* candle business in there.

2- The seat you pick on Day One is now your assigned seat. Move it, and you've just declared war on *Diane*.

3- Someone will cry. Someone will overshare. Sometimes it's the same person... sometimes it's you... and sometimes it's *Bathroom Brad* finally resurfacing.

4- Make eye contact with the facilitator? Congratulations, you're now the group spokesperson for *"feelings you didn't want to have today."*

5- If it's *Double-Down Debbie's* group, a newbie will storm out early. The rest of the group treats it like *March Madness*—brackets and all.

6- The *"I'm just listening today"* plan always ends with you trauma-dumping for ten minutes while everyone nods like they're on your podcast.

7- Laughter in group is medicine. Just... maybe not during someone's story about losing custody. (*Read the room, folks*)

8- What's said in group stays in group... unless it ends with, *"and that's why I can't go back to SeaWorld."*

9

I'm Not Like These People (Spoiler: You Are)

Almost everyone walks into rehab clutching the same secret thought like it's a VIP badge: I am not like these people. You tell yourself you are different. You just took one too many pain pills after surgery. You only drank wine on weeknights, which still counts as drinking. You had a stressful job, a bad breakup, *Mercury* was in retrograde. Whatever excuse helps you feel special. Surely you are not like that guy with meth-induced psychosis who has been living in the woods and swears he is married to a raccoon. But rehab is the great human equalizer. The second you are sitting in that same plastic chair, sipping the same burnt coffee, wearing the same stretchy sweatpants you swore you would never be caught dead in, the differences start to shrink. Suddenly, the pastor's wife who started with pain pills after a C-section has more in common with *Woods Guy* than either of them wants to admit. Because under the surface, it is not about the what, it is about the why. Everyone here was running from something.

At first, you hold onto your I am different card like it is a *Monopoly Get Out of Jail Free* pass. You sit in group mentally ranking your chaos against everyone else's. At least you never smoked meth. At least you did not lose custody of a parrot. At least you were not hiding your stash in a prosthetic leg. You nod politely at their stories while thinking that would never be me. Then one day someone shares a feeling, not a fact, a feeling that slices you open. Shame. Loneliness. That switch in your brain that will not flip off once you start. And it hits you like a bad cup of decaf: oh man, we are the same.

The lines blur fast. One day you are side-eyeing *Woods Guy* because he casually mentioned his raccoon wife. The next you are sitting next to him on smoke break wheezing with laughter because you both think the group trust fall exercise is stupid. The pastor's wife, who you swore was judging you, starts dropping jokes so filthy she would get banned from her own Bible study, and now you are laughing so hard you cannot breathe.

Rehab turns into this bizarre social experiment where the only membership requirement is that you have wrecked your life and now you are trying to duct-tape it back together. Once you see it, you cannot unsee it. Addiction does not care who you are. It does not care about your job, your degree, your *Peloton* streak, or how good you are at hiding vodka in a reusable water bottle. It is an equal-opportunity thief. And recovery is the same. It does not matter if you lost your soul in a church pew, a cubicle, or under a bridge. The way back is the same: honesty, humility, and the willingness to plop your butt down and admit, yes, *I am these people.*

Eventually, you start to feel lucky you are like these people. Because these people are hilarious. They are resourceful, the kind of resourceful where someone can create a phone charger out of a shoelace. They are brutally honest in ways the outside world never is. They will roast you for being fake and then hold your hand through a craving. They will clap for you like you just won *The Price Is Right* because you slept through the night. And that is the secret. It is not about the drug. It is about the hole you tried to fill with duct tape and bad decisions. Sitting there you wonder how the hell did all of us end up in the same room together. Different costumes, different stories, same hole, same fight. And maybe that is the point. None of us are as alone as we think. Here, everyone's story is different, but *the solution is the same.*

10 Signs You're Not as Different as You Think in Rehab:

1- You said, *"I'm not an addict, I just drink."* Cool — and I'm not broke, I just have *"creative banking."*

2- You act disgusted at people who stand in the cold smoking cigarettes... but by Tuesday you're outside at 2 a.m. selling your soul for a *Marlboro* butt.

3- You laughed at people who cry over a chip... now you hold your 30-day coin like it's the *Hope Diamond.*

4- You sneer at the girl who won't stop talking about crystals in group... but you knock on wood every time you say you're *"doing okay."*

5- You laugh at people begging for *Suboxone*... but you cried when the nurse wouldn't give you *Imodium.*

6- You call people *"pathetic"* for smoking meth... but your liver biopsy appointment is already on the calendar.

7- You smirked at the homeless guy with raccoon friends... but he had more loyalty than anyone you've ever had in your life.

8- You laughed at the girl who claps too hard in meetings... but you sulked when she didn't clap for you.

9- You said, *"I'm not like these people."* Funny — you're still in the same pajama pants, standing in the med line like the rest of us.

10- You sneered at the guy who robbed a gas station... but you've stolen your own kid's piggy bank money to buy a bottle of wine.

10

This Is Rehab, Not The Bachelor

Falling in love in rehab is like getting a tattoo on a sunburn. You can do it, but you probably should not. You show up three days sober, still sweating out last month's decisions, and suddenly there is that one person in group who *"just gets you."* You lock eyes during the *Serenity Prayer* and it feels like fate. You start mentally naming your future kids: *Paxil* and *Xanax Junior*. Rehab has a strange way of making everything feel cinematic. You are raw, vulnerable, and feeling actual feelings for the first time in a long time. Somebody hands you the hot sauce in the cafeteria and smiles, and suddenly you think it is destiny instead of the combined effects of detox and caffeine.

Before you ruin your discharge plan, hear me out. Rehab love is not real love. Rehab romances are trauma bonded speed runs. It is not *Netflix* and chill. It is trauma dump and chain smoke.

47

You are trying to build a house while the ground is still shaking under you. You are both rewiring your brains, untangling years of chaos, and trying not to cry because the instant coffee tastes like punishment. This is not the foundation for lifelong romance. This is an emotional earthquake.

Staff knows too. That is why they watch you like emotionally exhausted mall cops. The moment you sit too close to someone on the couch, here comes *Miss Betty* on night shift with her clipboard saying, *"Separate. Now."* They have been here long enough to know that the second two freshly detoxed people fall in love, someone is crying on the patio within twenty four hours. You will hear someone say, *"He listens to me. He really cares."* Girl, he really cares because he has no phone, no job, no outside stimuli, and no access to *TikTok*. You are not his soulmate. You are the only channel available. With enough boredom and monitored free time, even the wall starts looking supportive.

You will hear, *"We are getting a place together."* A place where. Neither of you has a credit score above 540, and one of you has a whole wife at home telling the pastor you are at a leadership retreat. Rehab love is like finding a puppy at a yard sale. You do not know where it came from, it is not trained, it is probably sick, and it will definitely urinate on everything you care about. You look at his wrists and whisper, *"There is just something about him."* Yes. There is. It is called pending charges.

If one of you gets discharged first, it becomes *The Titanic* instantly. Big tears, big promises, dramatic declarations like, *"I will wait for you Jack."* Honey, you live three hundred miles apart and cannot keep track of your vape. Let us calm down. By day three he is outside by the smoke pit whispering to a new girl named *Crystal* who has a *Stay Wild* tattoo and court papers tucked inside her Bible. He is telling her, *"You are different."* Of course she is. She is on day two of detox medications.

And when the rehab couple finally breaks up, which they always do, it turns the entire unit into a middle school cafeteria. She is crying on the patio with sunglasses on even though it is cloudy. He is pacing the hallway like a divorced dad outside a *Chuck E. Cheese.* And the best part is that they still have to sit in group together. The counselor asks, *"Would anyone like to share,"* and he is breathing like a bull at a rodeo while she is staring daggers into *Crystal.*

Here is the real problem with rehab romances. Your picker is broken. You are not drawn to what is healthy yet. You are drawn to what feels familiar. And in addiction, familiar often means dysfunctional with nice eyes. You are hungry for connection, so you latch onto the first thing that feels warm. Falling in love in rehab is like going grocery shopping while starving. You grab whatever looks good in the moment.

If you really want a shot at healthy love, wait until you have a life you are proud of. Build your routine, your stability, and your own version of happiness first. Then when you meet someone, they can be a partner, not a life raft. The truth is simple. The person you are supposed to fall in love with in rehab is you. Everyone else is just a background character in your origin story. Self respect is a lot sexier than whatever is happening in the lounge area at ten at night. Love can wait.

Your healing cannot. And you do not need a rehab boyfriend. *You need electrolytes.*

8 Signs Your Rehab Romance Is a Bad Idea:

1- You bonded over how much you both hate your counselor — because nothing says *true love* like mutual resentment.

2- Your "*dates*" are smoke breaks under the moonlight and they hand you the lighter like it's the candle ceremony on *The Bachelor.*

3- You've known each other exactly three days, and are already talking about moving in.

4- You're placed on a behavior contract and suddenly your roommate, *Big Country,* is running love notes for you like he's in the cartel.

5- You share cigarettes, secrets, and probably a counselor. (*And that's a love triangle nobody asked for*)

6- The biggest thing you have in common is that you both just learned what "*PAWS*" is.

7- Your idea of quality time is skipping group together and pretending it was "*self-care.*"

8- Everyone else in rehab has already placed bets on how long

you'll last — nobody said longer than 30 days.

11

My Emotions Showed Up Like: "Ma'am, We Have Been Trying To Reach You About Your Extended Warranty."

Most of us did not grow up learning what to do with feelings. We did not get *Emotional 101*. We got *"Go to your room,"* *"Quit crying,"* or *"Don't start."* Some of us had parents so stressed that if you even looked emotional, they got mad at you for it. When you grow up in that kind of world, you do not learn how to feel. You learn how to avoid. If your whole childhood taught you that big emotions create big consequences, with slammed doors, silent treatment, punishment, and chaos, then of course you learned to run from your own internal world. Of course you learned to stuff it, hide it, numb it, swallow it, fake it, minimize it. You were trained to. You did not learn emotional regulation. You learned emotional strategy. You became a tiny operator managing adult tempers, reading the room like a storm map, tracking the pressure systems in the people who were supposed to care for you. You did not develop a relationship with your own internal world. You developed a relationship with surviving theirs. You did not grow up thinking, *"How do I feel?"* You grew up thinking, *"Who is about to be mad, and do I need to hide behind the recliner?"*

Nobody teaches you how to feel safely. They just tell you to stop crying because you are making people uncomfortable. Which is confusing, because everyone else is making you uncomfortable, but you are the one who has to stop. We are raised to treat feelings like inconveniences. Happy is allowed. Everything else gets hidden, buried, silenced, or apologized for. Long before substances take over a life, emotional avoidance gets there first. The child who learns that sadness is too dramatic, that anger is disrespectful, that fear is weak, grows into an adult who believes they must silence themselves in order to be loved, accepted, or simply tolerated. They do not grow up learning how to feel. They grow up learning how to disappear.

And those feelings that were never allowed space, like grief, fear, loneliness, and shame, do not vanish. They wait. They collect. They stack. They press against the walls from the inside. And once adulthood arrives, those emotions become louder than the person who carries them. Addiction is not a story about pleasure. It is a story about escape. It is the story of someone who never learned how to feel without consequences. Someone whose emotional world was never met with safety, guidance, or compassion, only correction. So when a substance finally offered predictable relief, the brain grabbed onto it like a life raft. Addiction is emotional avoidance that turned into chemical dependence. Addiction did not walk in as a villain. It walked in as a solution. It said, "*I will take that feeling. I will quiet that fear. I will mute that memory. I will shut down that voice in your head. Just hand it over.*" And for a while, it worked. Until the cost became bigger than the relief.

Recovery is emotional literacy that turns back into freedom. It is learning that emotions are not evidence of weakness. They are evidence of being alive. They are signals. They are information. They are the necessary notifications of your nervous system saying, "*Something needs attention.*" Think of it like this. Your feelings are basically the dashboard lights on the busted *Honda Civic* that is your nervous system. Anxiety is your "*fifty miles till empty*" light. It is not a prophecy of doom. It is your brain saying, "*Hey buddy, you might want to pull over and put something in the tank before we end up praying on the side of I-16 again.*" Depression is your low tire pressure light. Slow, saggy, dragging you to the right like a *Walmart* cart with a bad wheel. It is not trying to ruin your life. It is saying, "*Hey champ, something is deflated in here. Pump it up before we are riding on the rim.*" Anger is your oil light. It is not a sign that you are a monster. It is your internal engine saying, "*Listen pal, I am about to set myself on fire. Please pour something helpful in me.*"

None of these lights are threats. They are signals. Little emotional mechanics tapping on the glass saying, "*Hey man, maintenance please.*" But when you ignore the lights long enough, when you white-knuckle the wheel and pretend you do not hear the knocking, that is when you end up broken down in flip-flops, thumb out, hitchhiking. And who pulls up? Your old buddy *Frankie Fentanyl* in a 1998 *Dodge Neon*. Windows down. Bass shaking. Two hubcaps missing. He leans over and says, *"Hop in bro, I missed you."* That is why feelings matter. They are not trying to kill you. They are trying to keep you from getting in *Frankie's* car again. The truth is simple. Your feelings were never trying to kill you. Your avoidance was.

So what now? You do not have to run from the feeling. You learn to let emotions exist. You let them speak long enough to understand what they are trying to tell you. *"Alright sadness, come sit on the couch. Do not touch my remote."* *"Okay anger, take a seat. Keep your shoes on."* *"Fine anxiety, you can come in too, but stay out of my kitchen because I just mopped, and stop reorganizing my spice rack."* Most emotions just want acknowledgment. Once they get it, they leave. No explosions. No disasters. Just truth, processed instead of buried. Just a *"Hey man, I see you, what's up?"*

This is the real miracle. Once you stop treating your emotions like enemies, they turn into guidance. They become the part of you that says, *"Pull over. Check in. Fix what needs fixing."* Not threats. Signals. Authentic internal intelligence.

10 Feelings *(And What They're Really Saying)*:

1- Anger: You're not actually furious about the group rule— you're furious you can't get high without losing custody again.

(Tell me I'm wrong)

2- Sadness: You don't miss *them*, you miss the chaos. Call a human being who won't ruin your credit score. *(Growth, baby)*

3- Anxiety: You think your counselor's squint means they don't believe you. They really just left their readers at home. *(Relax, you're not that interesting)*

4- Jealousy: That thing they have? It just proves it's possible. So go get your own instead of plotting their downfall. *(Yes, Becky, even you)*

5- Guilt: You're not carrying the sins of mankind—you just lied about doing your assignment. Sit down, *Judas. (We see you)*

6- Shame: You're not beyond saving—you just AMA'd for six hours in your head before staff reminded you that you had no ride or money. *(Classic)*

7- Contentment: This is the calm you used to call boring. Weird how not vomiting in a *Waffle House* parking lot feels like inner peace now. *(Namaste, y'all)*

8- Embarrassment: You think everyone's judging you, but nobody even remembers. They're too busy hiding their own dumpster fires. *(Congratulations, you're free)*

9- Suspicion: No one is plotting your downfall. They're literally just arguing over who hid the lighter. *(And you realize it was you, oops)*

10- Joy: You laugh so hard you snort... and then start laughing harder because you snorted, which turns into an asthma attack. *(10/10 would recommend)*

12

PAWS (And No, Not The Cute Ones)

PAWS stands for post-acute withdrawal syndrome. Post-acute simply means the withdrawal symptoms that show up after detox. The chemicals may be gone from your bloodstream, but your brain and nervous system are nowhere near finished. Detox clears the substances. *PAWS* is your brain learning how to function again without them.

And here is the part almost nobody understands: you are still withdrawing. You just do not realize these symptoms count.

I cannot tell you how many charts I read as a nurse that say, *"Patient has no withdrawal symptoms."* Then right underneath it will say anxiety seven out of ten, depression eight out of ten, irritability noted, cravings two out of ten. I stand there thinking, *Lord* help us, because even some medical professionals do not recognize *PAWS* when it is sitting right in front of them. That is how misunderstood this entire chapter of recovery is.

Most people only recognize detox withdrawal. If you are not shaking, sweating, vomiting, or climbing a wall like that girl from *The Exorcist*, everyone assumes, *"Well, I must be fine."* But you are not fine. You are withdrawing, just not in the dramatic, TV-movie way people expect.

When nobody teaches you what PAWS looks like, you walk around assuming something is wrong with you instead of understanding something completely normal is happening inside you.

That is why I hammer this point. If you do not understand PAWS, what it is, what it means, and what it does to the nervous system, you will mislabel your symptoms, under-report your needs, and gaslight yourself into believing you are overreacting. In reality, you are healing exactly the way a brain heals.

If you do not recognize PAWS, you cannot communicate your needs. And if you cannot communicate your needs, nobody can support you. Not the staff, not your family, not the people trying to help you, and not even you. And listen to me clearly. When you minimize your symptoms, the system assumes you are fine. Insurance believes the chart, not the chaos happening inside your nervous system. What you say and what you do not say matters more than you think.

The thing about PAWS is it does not follow rules. One morning you wake up ready to conquer the world, and by noon you have forgotten how to spell Wednesday. You will be telling a hilarious story in the lounge, killing it with the setup, and then halfway through, gone. The point just vanishes like your brain unplugged itself. And everyone is staring at you while you mumble, "*Uh... never mind.*" Meanwhile, your emotions are on a bad DJ setlist. One minute you are tearing up over a sad ballad, the next you are raving to techno with no transition at all.

And sleep? Forget it. Just as you are about to drift off, your legs start jerking and twitching like you are auditioning for *Riverdance*. Nothing makes you question your sanity quite like doing an *Irish* jig against your will at midnight.

PAWS is the period where your brain says, "*Alright, I have to start doing things myself again,*" and then struggles through the process. It is your brain trying to remember how to be a brain again.

Healing in real time is messy. Healing is loud. Healing will make you feel like you are losing your mind, but the truth is that you are getting it back piece by piece. And yes, PAWS takes months. Sometimes longer. Nobody loves hearing that, but rewiring takes time. That is simply how the nervous system works.

So let us break down the post-acute withdrawal symptoms people experience every single day, even though half of them swear they are completely fine.

Fatigue:

Your body is rebooting its entire dopamine system, and energy regulation is shot. Exhaustion hits even after doing nothing. Sleep does not fix it because your brain is rebuilding circuits behind the scenes like a stressed-out electrician. You ever been so tired your shadow looks tired? Like even it is walking a little behind you whispering, *"Yeah man... we are not doing too hot today."*

Mood Swings:

Without chemical regulation, your emotions swing harder than a toddler on a sugar high. Your limbic system is in the back room trying to recalibrate serotonin and dopamine with a blindfold on. One minute you are fine. The next you are crying because a *Dorito* broke wrong. Your own reflection looks back at you like, *"Girl... you good?"*

Anxiety:

The amygdala has been on a year-long rave and now it does not know when to chill. Everything feels like a threat because your body forgot what calm feels like. Sometimes my anxiety acts like a stray dog following me around. I am not feeding it, I am not talking to it, but it is right behind me like, *"Hey man... you got fear? You got any more fear?"* No buddy. Go home.

Depression:

The reward pathways in your brain are still rebooting. Pleasure and motivation feel muted. Your dopamine is whispering when it should be shouting, which makes everything feel heavy, flat, or pointless. Your depression walks around the house like a bored tour guide saying, *"And over here we have...*

nothing. Absolutely nothing you care about."

Obsessive Thinking:

Your brain is relearning how to regulate fear, reward, and uncertainty. Without substances muting the noise, your thoughts loop harder and longer than they need to. It is like your thoughts are on a treadmill they do not need to be on, and you are standing there saying, *"Who turned this on? Stop."*

Irritability:

Your brain is recalibrating stress hormones. Your tolerance is low. Your emotional fuse is short. Even small annoyances feel amplified. You ever get so irritable even your clothes feel disrespectful? Like, *"Why is this shirt touching me?"*

Insomnia:

Your internal clock is confused. Your brain is trying to regulate without substances and the timing is off for a while. My insomnia tucks me in like, *"Shhh go to sleep, baby,"* and then slaps me awake like, *"Psych."*

Brain Fog:

Your brain is rerouting and rebuilding. Focus, memory, and clarity glitch while your frontal cortex tries to take its job back from the part of you that used to run on impulse and survival mode. Sometimes the fog gets so thick you walk into a room and forget who you are, what you wanted, and why you are holding the microwave manual.

Emotional Numbness:

Your emotional wiring takes time to wake back up. After long periods of overstimulation or numbing, the *"feel something"* software takes a while to reboot. People are crying, confessing, arguing, breakdancing, and you are standing there like, *"Hmm. Interesting. Anyway."*

PAWS is a season. It is not a life sentence. It does not mean you are broken. It means you are coming back to life. Knowing what is happening inside your brain gives you power, and being able to communicate it gives you safety. With structure, support, patience, and real coping skills, you will come out the other side with something no substance ever gave you.

A nervous system that finally belongs to you again.

10 Common *PAWS* Symptoms You'll Have But Not Realize:

1- Symptom: Random Anxiety
Feels like you just got a text that says *"We need to talk"*... but from *God*. *(Terrifying)*
Survival Tip: Breathe, ground yourself, and remember—it's just your nervous system throwing a tantrum, not the *DEA* at your door.

2- Symptom: Concentration Issues
You sit down to start a Big Book assignment your counselor gave you, then spiral for 45 minutes about why *Pluto* isn't a planet anymore. *(Justice for Pluto)*
Survival Tip: Break tasks into toddler-sized pieces. Step 1:

pick up pen. Step 2: cry.

3- Symptom: Insomnia

Brain at 3 a.m.: *"What's your plan if a shark comes through the floor right now?"* *(Valid concern)*

Survival Tip: No caffeine after lunch, try a routine, and for the love of the *Discovery Channel*, stop watching *Shark Week* at bedtime.

4- Symptom: Memory Problems

You walked into the kitchen for water and walked out with a block of cheese, a lighter, and no recollection of your birth name. *(Relatable)*

Survival Tip: Sticky notes are your new bestie. Just don't forget where you stuck them, genius.

5- Symptom: Paranoia

You're dead sober but still acting like the FBI's parked outside your window in a white van. *(Classic)*

Survival Tip: Remind yourself: you're not that important. Nobody cares enough to watch you make your bed in rehab.

6- Symptom: Cravings

Your brain starts sounding like your ex: *"Come on, baby, you know you miss me."* *(Lies)*

Survival Tip: Call a friend. Trade the thought for candy. *Sour Patch Kids* never cheated on you.

7- Symptom: Mood Swings

One second: *"I love everyone here."* Next second: *"If Becky asks if I'm going to the meeting tonight like we have options, I'm burning her shower shoes." (Reasonable)*

Survival Tip: Don't make big decisions in your *"next second"* hours. Journal, walk, scream-sing into a pillow. Ask yourself: *"Is Becky worth a felony?"(Answer: no)*

8- Symptom: Depression

It sneaks in like that *iPhone* notification: *"You spent 9 hours stalking your ex's Instagram. You okay, champ?" (Absolutely not)*

Survival Tip: Move your body. Call a human. Or binge cat versus cucumber *TikToks* until you laugh hard enough to forget you exist.

9- Symptom: Overreacting

Burnt your toast? Cool, let's sell the house, divorce the spouse, and move to *Wyoming* to start a goat farm. *(Logical)*

Survival Tip: Ask: *Will this matter in 5 days?* No? Hush. Yes? Still hush. Nobody's buying you goats.

10- Symptom: Fatigue

You slept 16 hours and still woke up feeling like you got slapped by *Will Smith* at the *Oscars*, no commercial break. *(Keep my name out your mouth)*

Survival Tip: Move your body more. Hydrate. Don't fight it. Nap like it's your side hustle.

13

Cravings (The Hustler In Your Head)

Cravings do not tap politely. They slide in like a sleazy car salesman who has been waiting in the parking lot since 2009, loud, greasy confidence, sunglasses indoors, showing up saying, *"Ma'am, can I interest you in destroying your entire life again today? Do not answer, because I already wrote up the paperwork."* You will be having the most boring Tuesday, eating string cheese, paying bills, actually being a functioning adult, and then your own brain pops in like it is offering a deal on terrible choices: *"I am not saying we need anything. I am just saying it is an option."* An option. Like relapsing is the same as switching cell phone providers at *Costco*. Cravings do not want you high. They want your attention. They want you to look. They want engagement. Cravings feed on focus. The more attention you give them, the bigger they get, like an *Amazon* cart when you are sad. A craving is not the act. A craving is the lean.

I remember one day in early recovery when I was washing dishes at my sister's house. She was in the other room folding laundry, the TV was on low, nothing dramatic happening. And that is when I saw it, a prescription bottle on the window sill. Just sitting there. Doing nothing. Existing. And my brain snapped awake like a drug sniffing dog. I was not trying to take anything. I was not planning on stealing anything. What my brain wanted was much quieter than that. *"Just read the label, Julie."* It came as a sly whisper in my head, pretending it was harmless. *"Just see what it is, that is all."* I remember standing there pretending I was rinsing a plate, and every few seconds my eyes flicked back to that bottle like a magnet, like gravity, like muscle memory. For all I knew it could have been blood pressure medicine or antibiotics for the dog. I did not care what it was. I just felt my body wanting to engage the old ritual. Look. Think. Imagine. Touch. Open. *"Just one."* Then the freefall begins.

I physically turned my body away from the counter like a mother turning a toddler away from a socket because cravings do not want the relapse. They want the crack in the door. Once you crack that door, your brain will negotiate anything. So that day, I did not read the label. Not because I am cured. Not because I am strong. But because I finally understood the game. Cravings are like someone calling your phone from a number you used to answer. They do not stop calling. You just stop picking up. And that is recovery in the real world. Not a dramatic, noble war. Just a hundred tiny moments in random kitchens where you feel the old urge rise up and you choose yourself instead.

10 Dumb Lies a Craving Will Try to Tell Your Brain:

1- *"It's just this once."*
And so was *Adam and Eve's* little fruit moment — *God* heard that line before and invented consequences. Now we're all paying rent and fighting depression. Proceed accordingly.

2- *"You can handle it now."*
Right, and the *Titanic* could *"handle a little ice."* It couldn't.

3- *"You're strong enough to stop anytime."*
You also said that about *Target*, your vape, and your ex. Let's not test fate.

4- *"You'll make better choices this time."*
You once thought drinking on antibiotics was *"fine."* You're the cautionary tale *WebMD* warns about.

5- *"Everyone else does it."*
Everyone else also flosses and pays bills on time. You picking those habits up too?

6- *"It's not like last time."*
Facts. Last time you had a job, hope, and health insurance. *Blue Cross* bounced.

7- *"I just miss how it felt."*
And I miss when gas was $1.29, but here we are—broke, sober, and nostalgic.

8- *"One won't hurt."*

That's what *Jenga* players say right before a funeral for the coffee table.

9- *"You'll feel better instantly."*
   So does jumping out a window—for about three seconds.

10- *"Life's too boring without it."*
   You don't miss the feeling, you miss forgetting what feeling was. Welcome back to your frontal lobe; it missed you.

14

Coping Skills—Your New Superpowers (Because "Just White-Knuckle It" Is Not A Life Plan)

When I finally stopped using, I did not feel peaceful. I felt exposed. I felt like my skin did not fit right and every nerve ending in my body had been sanded down to live wire. In active addiction my coping skills were one step: avoid the feeling, sedate the feeling. Stress? *Use.* Fear? *Use.* Bored? *Use.* Celebrate? *Use.* My body got trained like a dog. Every emotional spike meant go get the chemical. My nervous system did not care about my goals. It cared about relief. So when the substance disappeared, I still had all the same emotional triggers with none of the chemical buffer.

Physical withdrawal ends long before rewiring does. Early recovery feels like this. You are sitting there sober with a full sized nervous system and zero equipment. It is like someone handed you a live grenade and said, *"Just do not pull the pin,"* and you are standing there thinking, *"Okay, but what do I do with my hands?"* Most people are not afraid of sobriety. They are afraid of being alone with their own interior world. Emotional detox is just as violent as chemical detox. You are not just detoxing a drug. You are detoxing your old reactions, your old reflexes, your old shortcuts. Without coping skills, you have no exit route. No alternative pathway. No bridge between intensity and calm. That is why people relapse. Not because they wanted the high, but because they had nowhere else for the feeling to go.

Coping skills are how you carve a new exit in your brain. They build trust with yourself. Every time you regulate instead of react, you prove you can be counted on. You are not learning coping skills because you are weak. You are learning coping skills because you are ending a chapter of emotional shortcuts. And honestly, coping skills are the actions that rewrite the next generation's nervous system map. Someone down the line will have less pain because you stayed calm today. That matters more than you think.

Most coping skills look insignificant. But the power is not the activity. It is the interruption. You are not trying to get peaceful. You are trying to stop escalation. Escalation is what detonates a whole life in a three minute window. It is wild how my brain will say, *"We are uncomfortable, want to burn our entire life down again?"* And a coping skill says, *"Or we could drink water."* It is insane that the choice is literally destruction or hydration, but those are the stakes.

Recovery is not about thinking positive. Recovery is about what you do with your body and mind when the urge hits. This toolbox is not theory. It is survival equipment. They all work differently, but every single one is evidence based and scientifically sound. They move you from reactivity to choice.

Below are the skills that saved me.

Future Visualization:
Future visualization is picturing yourself in the future sober, successful, maybe with a breed dog that does not bite people. You imagine yourself moisturizing your elbows, lighting the newly released fall candle from *Bath and Body Works*, and buying memory foam house slippers. You see peace. You see stability. You see a version of you who is thriving so hard that people from your past have to squint just to recognize you. That is future visualization. You give your brain a movie to chase so it stops replaying the horror film of your past.

HALT:
HALT is the simplest lifesaving coping skill out there: hungry, angry, lonely, tired. Those four conditions hijack your brain faster than any trigger ever could. You ever think you are having a spiritual crisis and then realize you just have not eaten since Tuesday? You thought you were being haunted. Turns out you just needed a *quarter pounder with cheese.* Hungry will have you ready to leave rehab, leave your marriage, leave Earth. Angry will have you ready to fight family members that are not even born yet, when really you are just dehydrated and petty. Lonely hits and suddenly you are like, *"I think I might marry my Uber driver. He just listened."* And tired will make you believe

the universe abandoned you, your ancestors abandoned you, and also your debit card keeps getting declined. Most *"I need to leave rehab right now"* moments are solved with a sandwich and a nap. Check those first before you diagnose yourself as spiritually doomed.

Goal Setting:

Goal setting gives direction. Without direction your brain defaults to chaos. You need somewhere to go or your body will wander back to where it used to be like a *Roomba* that keeps hitting the same corner convinced this time will be different. A brain without goals wakes up like, *"Well, guess I will ruin my life a little bit and see what happens."* A brain with goals stands up straighter, drinks water, and suddenly acts like it has a vision board and good credit. That is goal setting. You point your life in a direction so you do not accidentally stroll back into your old chaos like it is a clearance rack at *TJ Maxx.*

Mindfulness:

Mindfulness is learning to observe your thoughts instead of engaging them. You notice a meltdown brewing and you talk to your brain like, *"Hey girl, I can see your points are valid but not right now. I am exhausted and I already took my bra off."* It is not weakness. It is mastery. Mindfulness is sitting still watching your thoughts roll in like stray cats. You do not pet them. You do not feed them. You just say, *"Huh, that one is missing an ear."*

Stress Management:

Stress management is the preemptive strike. Relapse begins when stress accumulates unprocessed. Stress management is stopping your life from turning into a slow motion car wreck. Relapse does not start with cravings. It starts with stress stacking up like old mail on your counter and you keep walking past it thinking, *"That is not my problem,"* until suddenly it is your problem and your electric bill is eight hundred dollars. Stress pretends it is no big deal. Then out of nowhere you are ready to throw your phone, quit your job, and cut your own bangs with kitchen scissors. Managing stress is not cute or spiritual. It is practical. It is survival. It is noticing you are one inconvenience away from an emotional jailbreak and doing something before you snap. Because if you do not manage your stress, your stress will manage you.

Detachment:

"Not giving a sh**" is an underrated coping skill. Call it boundaries. Call it *"I am not letting Diane in group talk to me like I am her stepson again."* Detachment is when someone tries to drag you into chaos and you mentally clock out like, *"Not today."* It is when they start drama and you sip your water like it is witness protection. It is realizing you do not have to react or fix it and you definitely do not have to go to jail because *Diane* keeps pointing at you when she talks. It is that moment when someone tries to bait you into nonsense and you just stare at them with the same expression you use watching the microwave count down. Emotionless. Timeless. Spirit somewhere else. Full detachment mode activated. Call it peace. Call it maturity. Call it the only reason *Diane* still has all her teeth.

Gratitude:

Gratitude is not denial. It is recalibration. It is your brain saying, "*Maybe not everything is garbage.*" Gratitude shifts the vibe from "*I am doomed and the universe hates me and Diane is plotting on my downfall*" to "*Alright, the coffee was decent today and my pants still fit.*" Gratitude drags your brain out of its dramatic soap opera and reminds it to look at what is still here, not just what hurts. Tiny wins. Big impact. Reality with better lighting.

Time Management:

Time management keeps your day from becoming one long open hallway full of relapse opportunities. Empty hours are danger zones. When you have nothing to do, that is when your brain gets ideas. Not good ideas. Structure does not control you. Structure protects you. When you schedule your day, you are telling your addiction, "*Sorry, I am booked. I do not have a single time slot available to destroy my future right now.*" If you do not give your time a job, your past will give it one. And your past does not care about your recovery.

Exercise:

Movement clears your mind, regulates your mood, and gives your brain actual energy. Exercise is trauma metabolism. When you move your body you burn off adrenaline, cortisol, and all the stress chemicals buzzing around your bloodstream like psychotic bees. People think motivation causes movement. It does not. Movement causes motivation. If we waited to feel inspired, we would still be lying on the couch eating *Takis* and scrolling *TikTok.* One brisk walk and your brain says, "*Is this what healthy people feel like? Do I buy a blender now?*" It is wild. The solution to feeling terrible is making your body feel terrible for fifteen minutes with a side of shin splints so your brain can feel amazing. It does not make sense. But neither does anything else in life, so just go with it. Your trauma would love nothing more than to stay stored in your hamstrings forever. Do not let it.

Play the Tape Through:

"*Play the tape through*" makes you watch the real ending. The one you already know. The one you swore on your mama's recliner you would never repeat. "*Play the tape through*" ruins the vibe the way old *Snapchat* memories ruin your self esteem. Absolutely not. That ending sucks. Always has. Always will. That is why you play the tape through. It kills the fantasy before the fantasy kills you.

Enjoyable Activities:

Activities you enjoy are how you rewire pleasure. Joy is relapse prevention. Healthy dopamine matters. If your life has zero joy, your brain says, "*For what reason am I staying sober? To stare at beige walls and pay bills?*" Give your brain something to look forward to. A hobby. A trashy reality show. A treat like the rectangle pizza from middle school. Your brain needs that same level of anticipation to stay alive. If nothing in your life feels good, why would your brain choose to stay? You have to give it reasons. Tiny ones. Silly ones. Delusional in a charming way ones. That is healthy dopamine. You train your brain to enjoy safe things so it stops sprinting back to the dangerous ones.

Thought Challenging:

This is when you tell your brain, "*Hey man, that is a big*

accusation. You got proof?" When your brain goes, *"Everyone hates you,"* you say, *"Name three."* Your brain fires back, *"Diane, Big Country, and that mean counselor."* You say, *"Alright, facts, I will give you those three. Now name five."* Suddenly the brain goes silent because even your anxiety knows it was being dramatic. That is thought challenging. You make your brain show the receipts and half the time it cannot finish the list.

Radical Acceptance:

Radical acceptance is when you stop fighting reality and accept that your life is the *Temu* version of what you ordered on *Amazon.* You pictured yourself in a tailored blazer strutting into court like *Olivia Pope. Temu* delivered you a blazer sized for a slightly overweight four year old. And instead of crying, you put your adult arms through those toddler armholes, say *"It is what it is,"* and march into the courthouse with your elbows sticking out like a confused chicken nugget. It is not glamorous. It is not what you wanted. But you are wearing it anyway.

Grounding (5 Senses):

Grounding resets the body from threat mode into presence mode. It is when you look around the room like you have been kidnapped and are memorizing details for your *Dateline* interview. *"Yes officer, I remember everything. The clock said 12:01. The air smelled like Great Value coffee. My hand touched something wet. Do not ask questions. In the distance I heard what I thought were baby monkeys crying. Turned out it was group therapy. Same energy. And there was a metallic taste in the air like I licked a handful of pennies."* That is grounding. You are not calm. You are observant. You snap your brain out of panic by paying attention to the moment. You are ready for *Lester Holt*.

Social Contact:

Pre loading your lifelines is strategy. Sometimes you need to call someone whose mental health is stronger than yours. Call *Angie*. *Angie* will answer mid *Costco* run, hear your whole emotional collapse, and still tell you which probiotic you need. She will say, "*Okay breathe. Not like that. You sound like you are in labor. Try again.*" She will talk you off the ledge and then say, "*So anyway, I saw Ashley's fifth ex husband at Dollar Tree buying reading glasses and a pregnancy test.*" Because distraction is therapy. Call *Angie*. She knows your crazy and loves you anyway.

Structured Rest:

Sleep is a legal drug. Every time you nap you wake up like a newborn calf wondering where you are. You take a forty seven minute nap and wake up thinking, "*Is it morning? Did I miss work? Am I married? Why does my mouth taste like drywall?*" Structured rest is letting your brain reboot so you stop acting like the villain in your own story and start acting like someone who has had a sandwich. You lay down. You go unconscious. You wake up spiritually refreshed and physically confused.

Spirituality:

Spirituality is not religion. It is connection to something bigger that gives pain meaning. Meaning is how the nervous system tolerates discomfort without escape. Even if all you can do is whisper, "*Help me get through this,*" that is still a connection. That still counts. You do not need a burning bush or a chakra chart. Sometimes spirituality is sitting on the edge of your bed saying, *"If anybody out there is on shift, please clock in. Your girl is struggling."* It is not about perfection or rituals or pretending to be enlightened when you barely survived group therapy without flipping a table. It is about connection. A tiny human thread that reminds you that you are not doing this alone.

Urge Surfing:

Urge surfing is riding your cravings like a mechanical bull at a county fair where the operator still remembers you kissed his girlfriend in fifth grade and wants you gone. It is holding on while the bull launches you like a *Walmart* lawn chair in a hurricane. You grip the handle and say, *"You are not knocking me off, Jimmy John. Not today."* Urges peak. They wobble. They get tired. They give up. You ride it out and breathe. The bull always stops bucking.

Music Regulation:

Music will regulate you better than *Lexapro*. *Billie Eilish* is cheaper than your antidepressant copay, zero deductible, one hundred percent vibes. One song can change your personality. You put on *Lizzo* saying she is one hundred percent that bit** and suddenly you remember you are too. You block fifty people on Instagram, stand up straighter, and pay your car insurance on time. That is music regulation. Your brain says, *"Therapy?"* and the playlist says, *"I got it."*

Deep Breathing:

Deep breathing is not fancy. It is inhaling like you are trying to figure out who microwaved fish in the staff lounge, then exhaling slow like you are blowing into a breathalyzer trying to convince the universe you are sober and also a good person. The exhale is the important part. When it is longer than the inhale, your vagus nerve hits the brakes on your panic the same way a mom slams her arm across your chest when she stops the car too fast. It looks stupid. It feels stupid. But it works. It gets your thinking brain back online so you stop treating everything like a five alarm emergency. Breathe in peace. Blow out chaos. And your nervous system leans back like, *"Thank God. I thought we were about to run into traffic."*

There is no universal coping skill that works for everyone. Your job is to learn your nervous system's menu. What calms you down. What grounds you. What gets your thinking brain back online. People get sober because they learn how to tolerate the moment long enough to choose something else. The moment is everything. Coping skills are moment management tools. You do not need to solve your whole story. You just have to regulate this moment. Recovery is not about never getting overwhelmed again. It is about having actual tools so when your nervous system tries to hijack you, you do not hand your life back to the thing that almost killed you. Coping skills are not the backup plan. They are the plan. Because one day you will catch yourself feeling a feeling and not destroying anything over it and you will think, *"Wait, who am I?"* You are a person with options now. And that is the whole point.

10 Coping Skills They Don't Teach You in School *(But Actually Work in Recovery)*:

1- Sitting in the *Target* parking lot with an iced coffee, pretending it's therapy — because honestly, sometimes it is.

2- Screenshotting a fight, zooming in on their typo, and letting THAT be your closure. (*"You said your instead of you're, case closed."*)

3- Writing your anger down so it's on paper, not on your rap sheet.

4- Singing *Let It Go* in *Elsa's* voice every time you catch yourself spiraling. Extra points if you throw in the hand twirl.

5- Making your bed just so you don't climb back into it like depression's favorite employee of the month.

6- Driving around with your sober friend, radio blasting, both of you tag-teaming *Push It* like *Salt-N-Pepa* on a *Honda Civic* comeback tour.

7- Watching true crime not for the crime, but to roast the criminals' bad decisions like *"bro left fingerprints at the scene?? Amateur hour."*

8- Breaking up with your cravings in a letter: *"It's not me, it's literally you. Don't text."*

9- Rearranging your furniture at 2 a.m. like *HGTV* is filming you. New room, new me.

10- Laughing at yourself — because if you don't, your probation officer probably will.

15

Called Out, Cleaned Up (When Someone Finally Says What You've Been Avoiding)

There is a special kind of honesty in rehab, the kind you cannot find in the wild. It is blunt, sacred, disrespectful, lifesaving, and somehow tender. Someone looks you dead in the eye and says, "*That is bullsh**,*" and instead of getting offended, a small part of your soul whispers, "*Finally.*" Outside, people tiptoe around your mess. Inside rehab, nobody has the glucose for that. Everyone is detoxing, everyone is triggered, and everyone is too tired to babysit your ego.

Rehab honesty hits you like a folding chair in the *WWE.* Pride goes limp. Ego taps out. At first you get mad. You sit there with your arms crossed like you are in a *JCPenney* portrait thinking, "*They do not know me.*" Imagine you are mid-dramatic monologue. *Your voice is shaking. Brenda is rubbing your back like you are auditioning for a tragic movie role.* You drop the line: *"No one has ever truly loved me."* You wait for the gasps. But the quiet woman, the one who has not spoken in three weeks, looks up, takes a slow breath, and says, *"Sweetheart, the only person who has never loved you is you."* Boom. Mic drop. Someone gasps. Someone crosses themselves. Someone whispers, *"Oh Lord."* Group ends early. You ascend three inches above your chair. Even your dead grandmother sat up like, *"Finally. Someone told her."*

Rehab honesty is a weapon of mass transformation. It should require a permit. It is weirdly holy, violently supportive, and deeply uncomfortable in the exact way change is supposed to be. Your detox buddy *Ashley* flops into her seat like a *Victorian* widow, unwraps a warm *Werther's Original*, and says, *"I don't know why this keeps happening to me."* Twelve strangers who cannot agree on breakfast but can agree on this respond in perfect harmony: *"You do. You just don't want to look at the part you play in it."* And not one of them looks sorry.

Then one guy stands up like, *"Alright, I'll say it."* He says, *"You are bossy, manipulative, and mean. You wear way too much eyeliner. And if you click that candy in your teeth one more time, I am throwing out everything you smuggled in here in the first place."* The counselor does not intervene because it is better therapy than anything they can bill *Blue Cross* for.

It is honesty that stops you in your tracks because, for the first time, someone is telling you the truth instead of what you want to hear. It is like discovering a wrinkle you never noticed.

Terrifying. But empowering. And here is the wildest twist: you do not hate him. You love him. You love him like someone just pulled you out of a river. Because they did. They saved you from yourself. If they did not think you were capable of better, they would let you drown in your delusion.

These people are not trained. They do not have degrees. They have lived experience and poor boundaries. That is even worse. And somehow it works. Because you cannot lie to these people. They have lied to judges, probation officers, landlords, the IRS, and sometimes *God* Himself. You do not stand a chance. *Angie* says, "*Baby, if three frogs croak at you, maybe you are the swamp.*" *Big Country* goes, "*Now hold on, I ain't trying to be rude, but that right there is some Grade A bullsh**.*" And *Spider*, who once died for eight minutes in a *7-Eleven* bathroom and came back with clarity, leans in and says, "*You don't choose you. That is why nobody else does. Everyone else was simply following your lead.*"

You feel it in your bones. In your soul. In whatever is left of your serotonin. And you sit there stunned because it is true. You do not get mad. You get relieved. Being called out is love with a backbone. Outside rehab, people are terrified of upsetting you. Inside rehab, people are terrified of you *dying*.

And then the transformation hits. You stop running from honesty. You start chasing it. You stop panicking when someone calls you out. You lean in and say, "*Say it again, but clearer.*" You stop hiding behind stories. You drag your own lies into the light. That is the shift. You start calling yourself out. "*I am exaggerating.*" "*I am avoiding the real issue.*" "*That*

85

was not the truth, that was the remix." "I am being dramatic. Let me run that back."

That is healing. That is the moment rehab stops happening to you and starts happening through you. It is the miracle. It is the moment you finally realize that being called out was not people hurting you. It was people saving you. And the day you hear the truth and whisper, *"Thank you, I needed that,"* that is maturity. That is restoration. You are not ruined because you were called out. You are restored because someone cared about you enough to say the thing you could not yet say to yourself.

10 Ways You Know You're About to Get Called Out:

1- Someone in group takes a deep breath and says, *"So... here's the thing."* Translation: it's about to be your thing.

2- Your counselor tilts their head like a confused golden retriever. You're about to get fetch'd.

3- *"I don't want to call anyone out, but..."* Congratulations, you've just been called out.

4- Someone says your name followed by, *"With all due respect..."* and you know respect just left the building.

5- *"I'm just speaking generally..."* Nope. They mean specifically. About you.

6- You hear, *"I'm just gonna be honest..."* and immediately regret existing.

7- Your friend starts with, *"I love you, but..."* and you know love is not about to win.

8- *"No offense to anyone, but—"* Buckle up, because offense is already pulling into the driveway.

9- You feel your stomach drop and think, *"Oh no... they know."* *(Girl, we been knew)*

10- The tech starts the sentence with, *"Not to single anyone out..."* — Congrats, you're the single, the duet, and the whole choir.

16

Triggers —(Why That Random Smell, Song, Or Tuesday Can Mess With Your Head)

In recovery, triggers are not enemies to fear. They are echoes to understand, quiet reminders that your brain once confused survival with self-destruction. A smell, a song, a stretch of sunlight across a sidewalk, and suddenly something in you stirs. It is not danger. It is memory. It is the body remembering what the mind has finally outgrown. A trigger is *déjà vu* with bad intentions. It sneaks up behind you like, *"Hey, remember how good that felt?"* Oh, do I? You mean the night I thought I was the star of a music video but actually looked like I had lost custody of both my mascara and my dignity? Yes. Magical times.

Triggers slide into your *DMs* wearing nostalgia and cheap

perfume. One whiff of that cologne your ex wore during your codependent circus era and your nervous system suddenly starts doing jazz hands. Or maybe you hear a beer can open in a movie and your brain says, *"I wonder what my old bar is up to."* Girl, it is still sticky. Someone is still onstage singing karaoke with a vape in one hand and unpaid child support in the other. Nothing changed except your self-respect.

Triggers do not mean you are weak. They mean your brain is doing spring-cleaning with a hangover, pulling out old emotional crop tops that do not fit anymore. And this is where your actual power starts. *Name them. Claim them. Do not entertain them.* When that memory stirs, do not shame it. Witness it. You are not weak for feeling it again. You are wise for noticing it this time.

The moment you say, *"This is just a trigger,"* the whole thing changes shape. It goes from a monster you need to run from to a toddler with a foam sword. Naming a trigger strips off its costume. You shift from *"What is wrong with me?"* to *"Oh, this is that feeling."* So when a trigger hits, do not panic and do not spiral. Narrate it like *David Attenborough* describing wildlife: *"Ah yes, the recovering human encounters a wild memory. Observe as she takes a deep breath and does not text her ex."*

Every trigger is a test of recognition, not resistance. You do not have to fight them. You only have to see them. Every time you recognize one and do not follow it, you are rewiring your power. You are teaching your brain, *"Nice try, but we are not doing that rerun again."* Recovery is not about erasing the past. It is about outgrowing its authority. You will still get reminders, songs, smells, familiar faces, and people who think *Facebook* is therapy. But they will bounce off you instead of dragging you back.

And one day you will pass that bar, hear that song, smell that cologne, and keep walking. Maybe you will even smile, because the same thing that once hijacked your sanity now reminds you how far you have come.

10 Weird Things That Can Trigger You:

1- The sound of handcuffs clicking on *Law & Order* — instant flashback, free PTSD included.

2- The ice machine at *Motel 6* — because nothing good ever happened while waiting on those cubes.

3- That one *Chili's* commercial jingle — because nothing triggered cravings like *"baby back ribs"* at rock bottom.

4- Seeing a police car behind you, heart rate instantly at 200, even though the wildest thing in your cup holder is a *Diet Coke*.

5- Someone cracking a soda can and your brain going, *"We still doing this or nah?"*

6- Hearing the *Nickelback* song *Rockstar* and realizing... not everybody does have a drug dealer on speed dial.

7- The smell of county jail bologna — haunting, specific, unforgettable.

8- The squeak of a lighter wheel — *Pavlov's* bell for your whole nervous system.

9- *Facebook Marketplace* posts that start with *"Needs gone today."*

10- *Walgreens* pharmacy text: *"Your prescription is ready for pickup."*

17

Complete Honesty Equals Complete Freedom

When you're living in addiction, honesty is... flexible. Like yoga-teacher flexible. You become part-time novelist, part-time magician, spinning stories, pulling rabbits out of excuses, making entire weekends disappear. And you start thinking, damn, I might actually be good at this.

Until one day you realize you've lied so much you need a *PowerPoint* just to keep your stories straight. You're running a whole underground operation: aliases, alibis, witness-protection-level planning. You don't even know if your dog's real name is *Buddy* or *Brenda*.

Then recovery rolls in like, *"Hey, we're gonna tell the truth now,"* and your first reaction is, *"Absolutely not. That sounds horrible."*

But here's the thing: lying is exhausting. It's like juggling chainsaws blindfolded while pretending you're fine. Recovery flips it. Suddenly telling the truth is easier. You don't have to remember who got which version of *"my car broke down"* versus *"my aunt had surgery for her sixth toe."* You just say the thing. And you're done.

No rehearsing, no dodging people in the hallway like a secret agent in flip-flops. Just the truth. Clean, simple, kind of terrifying, but weirdly freeing.

At first, honesty feels like handing people bullets and turning around like, *"Please don't shoot me."* But then you realize when you own your mess, nobody can use it against you. You already aired your dirty laundry. Hell, you hung it out front and used scent beads.

And then comes the best part: telling the truth is lazy-person friendly. No fact-checking texts. No mental spreadsheets. No panic attacks when someone says, *"Wait, didn't you say...?"* You can finally just exist. Honesty is freedom. Not the *Instagram*-quote kind, the real, *"Wow, I can actually breathe again"* kind.

When you stop performing, stop curating, stop trying to manage what everyone else thinks, you get to be the same person in every room. You don't have to shapeshift to survive. You just show up as your beautifully awkward, slightly sweaty, coffee-stained self.

That's authenticity. When you stop chasing *"impressive"* and start living *"undeniably you."* Because people don't connect with perfect. They connect with real. And "*real*" sometimes smells like *Dollar Tree* deodorant (don't knock it, *PowerStick* got me through 2014) and microwave burritos, but it moves mountains.

It's power through imperfection. It's courage that hasn't seen a hairbrush in two days but still showed up to change its life. Easy? Nah. Sometimes you've got to tell your inner child, "*Not every bad boy with prison tat and potential is your soulmate. Some just end up getting you 180 community service hours.*" (Long story.)

But every time you tell the truth, a little bit of shame flakes off like dead skin during one of those exfoliating-glove showers where you question every decision you've ever made. You get lighter. You get freer. You glow. And eventually the truth feels so good, you can't imagine going back. Pretending then feels like pulling *Spanx* up on your soul. But once you're living in full honesty, you're not keeping anything stuffed in anymore; you're walking, hair wild, heart steady, vibe feral, straight into your freedom.

When I got home from rehab, I called my ex-husband to ask if I could see the kids. He said no. Old me would've begged, defended, cried, probably thrown in a guilt trip for good measure. But this time I just said, "*Okay.*"

That threw him off. He was ready for the old script. You know, the one where he got to play the reasonable victim and I played the emotional disaster. So he pushed.

"You don't realize all you've done," he said.

  "I do," I told him.

  "You were a terrible mother."

  "I was."

  "And a terrible wife."

  "I was that too."

  "You're still an addict."

  "Yes, I am."

He went quiet, angry, confused. Finally he snapped, *"Stop being a smart ass, Julie."*

"I'm not," I said. *"I agree."*

And that was it. No screaming, no defending, no tears. Just silence. For the first time in our entire relationship, there was nothing left to argue about.

That's what honesty does. It ends wars that used to take up whole chapters of your life. When you own your story, no one can use it against you. The truth becomes armor. And peace starts sounding a lot like power.

When you stop defending your past, it stops defining you. People can only shame you with the parts of yourself you haven't forgiven yet. Once you make peace with those pieces, there's nothing left for them to aim at. Accountability is something I give freely. Shame is not.

You want to talk about what I did?
Great. I'll tell it better.

You want to remind me who I was? Thank you. She's the reason I'm who I am now.

Your past isn't a weapon in someone else's hand anymore. It's fuel in yours.

You become someone not controlled by shame. You become empowered by lessons.

Mic dropped. Probably dented. *Worth it.*

10 Perks of Radical Honesty:

1- You no longer panic when your sponsor, your counselor, and your baby mama all end up in the same *Applebee's*.
(You just take the mic, order wings, and say, "Since we're all here... ")

2- You don't flinch when someone says *"truth or dare."*
  (Truth is the dare now)

3- You feel free when admit the real reason you shaved your head wasn't *"a fresh start"*—it was lice in county jail. *(Not gonna lie... it made you look like you ran that cell block)*

4- People slowly start trusting you again... like a cat sniffing a new human. Suspicious, but progress.

5- Your memory upgrades instantly—because you're no

longer juggling a whole *Marvel* multiverse of nonsense backstories.

6- No more telling your kid, "*It's adult business*" when really it was just you being shady.

7- You get to watch people's faces when you actually tell the truth — it's comedy gold.
(You'll never top the reaction to, "Yeah, I stole your charger and your boyfriend, Sharon.")

8- You can both stop pretending the thermostat war at home is about comfort. It's about control. Always has been.

9- At work, you can stop fake-typing when your boss walks by. Now you just smile and wave.

10- You get the underrated joy of shrugging and saying, "*Yep, I did that*," instead of performing a full courtroom defense in the *Walmart* parking lot.

18

If You Want a Doormat, Go to Home Depot

I did not grow up understanding boundaries. If someone mentioned them in treatment, I honestly pictured property lines. Something official. Something scenic. Maybe a white fence. Definitely not something I possessed. I thought boundaries were gentle conversations where you touched someone's elbow and said, "*Could you maybe stop ruining my life? If that's okay?*" Basically, a polite suggestion.

That is not what boundaries are. Boundaries are "*no*," said with your chest. They are the emotional version of installing a *Ring* camera on your soul. If you have spent your whole life letting people treat you like a spiritual *DoorDash*, saying no feels illegal. You feel like someone is going to appear out of the ceiling tiles with a clipboard and say, "*Ma'am, we are going to need you to come with us. You just told someone no.*"

I grew up my whole life saying yes because I thought that was what good people did. Good daughters. Good friends. Good partners. Good hostages. Recovery peeled my life apart like an orange and showed me the truth: I had spent years letting people climb me like a jungle gym and then wondered why my ribs hurt.

Someone asked me for a "*favor.*" And by "*favor,*" I mean: can you say yes to something you have already said no to in your spirit. Normally I would have said, "*Sure, anything, do you also need a kidney while I am at it?*" because I thought people liking me was my whole personality. Everything in my nervous system screamed, say yes or you will die alone in a *CVS* parking lot.

But something rose up in me that day. Was it self-worth? Was it spiritual awakening? Was it the *Zoloft*? We may never know. But I said, "*I cannot do that.*" And that person literally said, "*Okay.*" No thunder. No lightning. No SWAT team. *Nothing.*

I stood there like I had unlocked a cheat code. Like the universe whispered, welcome to *Level 2*. It felt like someone handed me a key to a house I had been living in my whole life but never knew had doors. I said no and suddenly I was checking the sky for helicopters like, "*Oh wait, am I allowed to do that?*" Because if you grew up people-pleasing, feeling guilty is your love language.

But I started saying no to nonsense with the confidence of a cat knocking things off a shelf while maintaining eye contact. Every no becomes a yes to something holy. Peace. Rest. Tacos.

99

Sitting in blessed silence while nobody asks you for anything. Once you say no one time, suddenly your brain is like, *"Wait, so we do not have to do things we hate?"*

Does it feel weird at first? Absolutely. You will feel guilty. You will over-explain. You will walk away thinking, *"Did I just ruin Christmas?"* But eventually, you get there. One day you say, *"No, thanks,"* without sweating, shaking, or apologizing. No, I will not go to your cousin's birthday dinner at *Applebee's.* No, I am not lowering my standards to make you comfortable. No, I will not drive across town to help you find your vape. No, I will not explain myself, *Susan.*

A boundary says, I know who I am now. I know what I can hold. I know what my spirit cannot survive anymore. A boundary says, if you cannot meet me with honesty and respect, then this is your stop. The bus does not go further. A boundary says, love me correctly or lose access.

Boundaries do not need a *PowerPoint* presentation. They do not need softening. They do not need a backstory. They do not need to be wrapped in twenty-seven versions of sorry. Boundaries are not walls. Walls keep everyone out. Boundaries are doors with locks. They protect the version of you who is actually trying. They protect your recovery. They protect your peace. They protect you from becoming a person who smiles on the outside and resents everyone on the inside.

Healthy people will respect your no. Unhealthy people will act like you personally ruined their entire bloodline. *"I miss the old you."* Translation: *"I miss the version of you who required nothing from me and tolerated everything.*"

Repeat your boundary like you are glitching.
Them: "*But why?*"
You: "*I cannot do that.*"
Them: "*Can you think about it?*"
You: "*I cannot do that.*"
Them: "*But what about—*"
You: "*Still no.*"
Them: "*What if—*"
You: "*No.*"
Them: "*I am really disappointed in you.*"
You: "*Okay. Still no.*"

You become the human version of a vending machine that ate someone's dollar. It is not personal. It just is not happening. People will get mad. That is fine. People get mad that *Chick-fil-A* closes on Sundays. It does not mean *Chick-fil-A* is wrong.

No is not dramatic. No is holy. No is your inner child gripping your hand and whispering, "*Please do not abandon me again.*" No is the moment your healing finally outweighs your fear of losing people who were never holding you in the first place.

And once you start saying it, something dangerous happens. You become someone who cannot be manipulated. Someone who cannot be guilted. You become someone who chooses themselves on purpose, without apology and without flinching, like a human who finally realized their superpower is not being liked but being unbothered.

101

No is not mean. No is maintenance. And if someone gets mad that you stopped letting them drain you, let them. Because someone being mad that you finally respected yourself is the biggest red flag since the *Titanic* left the dock. They will live. And for the first time ever, so will you.

Because no is not rejection. No is protection. No is self-respect stepping into the room and saying, move, I got it from here.

Beginner's Guide to Saying No Without Imploding:

1- The Polite Deflection
   "*I can't right now, but thank you for asking.*"
   Translation: I'm shutting the door, not leaving you a window.

2- The Broken Record
   Just keep saying "*I can't*" until they either give up or call 911.

3- The Tacos Over Trouble Rule
   If the choice is between drama and tacos, you already know.

4- The Schedule Shield
   "*Sorry, I already have plans.*"
   Plans = couch, crumbs, *Hulu*, zero shame.

5- The Honest Hit
   "*That doesn't work for me.*"
   Period. No further explanation. I'm not submitting a thesis.

6- The Reverse *Uno* Card

*"Actually, can you help me move a couch?"*Poof—they're gone.

7- The Recovery Card

*"That would put my recovery at risk."*Checkmate. Nobody argues with that.

8- The Power of Silence

Say "no," then stare. Watch them sweat like the last block in a *Jenga* tower.

9- The Over-the-Top Honesty

"That sounds like a straight-up nervous breakdown starter pack, so no."

10- The Straight-Up *"No"*

No smile, no apology, no guilt. Just no.
(*Warning: strangely addictive once
   you start*)

19

Speaking Fluent Recovery-ese

There is a moment in recovery when you suddenly realize you are speaking a language you were never consciously taught. It slips in quietly, the way bad decisions do, except this time it saves your life instead of ruining it. One minute you are communicating like a normal civilian, and the next you are standing in *Publix* telling the cashier that you are just taking it as it comes. She smiles and says, *"Love that, buy one get one today, huh,"* completely unaware that you are spiritually negotiating with the universe, not the price of the *Ben and Jerry's.* You do not choose *Recovery-ese.* It chooses you. It adopts you. It taps you on the head and says, *"Welcome, chosen one. Here are your phrases. Use them wisely."*

It starts small. You drop a *"letting go of what I cannot control"* while circling the parking lot searching for a space. You hear yourself say *"progress, not perfection"* while battling a fitted sheet that clearly hates you. Inside rehab, these sayings make perfect sense. If you say, *"I am staying in my lane,"* everyone nods because they, too, have crashed headfirst into emotional traffic. If your roommate is crying because she got put on a behavior contract and you whisper, *"This too shall pass,"* she looks at you like you just handed her a sacred scroll.

It is not only the phrases. It is the tone. In rehab, you can say *"Feelings are not facts"* in a calm, mystical voice and the entire room will stop and breathe. Try saying that to your cousin when he is ranting about the *Falcons* losing and watch how quickly he tells you to hush. Say it in the outside world. Tell your aunt, *"I am living life on life's terms,"* and she will look at you like you joined that secret cult that meets at *Mattress Firm* on Saturday nights. Say, *"This too shall pass,"* and your family acts like you just foreshadowed a storm in the distance. Your dad will glance out the window searching for clouds. You start sounding like a wise monk or an extremely confused weather reporter. People will either see you as enlightened or unwell. It depends on the lighting.

The true absurdity hits when you whisper, *"I cannot control the outcome, only my actions,"* while the McDonald's employee informs you that the ice cream machine is down in a tone that suggests it has never once been up in the history of *America*. You are offering spiritual guidance while someone is simply trying to decide if they should buy a new couch from *Wayfair*. *Recovery-ese* works in the real world, but it lands differently. Out there, people think it is motivational-poster nonsense. Inside you, it is a survival operating system. It is how you got here. It is how you stayed here. It is how you stopped throwing your life against the wall like spaghetti.

Eventually, you learn to translate. Instead of telling your non-recovery friend, *"Let go and let God,"* you say, *"Girl, stop trying to control everything. You are not the manager of the universe."* Instead of *"This too shall pass,"* you say, *"It will not feel like this forever."* You keep the soul, but you take out the secret rehab handshake.

But here is the truth. You will always keep a little *Recovery-ese* on you. Just a pocketful. Like spiritual pepper spray. So if a stranger at the dentist office thinks you are odd for accidentally yelling *"Keep coming back"* as they walk out, let them think it. They do not know that phrase once saved your life.

People on the outside think *"Easy does it"* is something cute you stitch on a decorative pillow. They have no idea that *"Easy does it"* is the only reason that when my boss said, *"Just warning you, I am in a bad mood today,"* I did not respond with, *"Well, I am in a petty mood, so proceed at your own risk."* They do not understand that these sayings are not inspirational posters to us. They are survival tools. They kept us from throwing hands, sending unhinged texts, or quitting jobs on our lunch breaks with our name tags still warm.

Let them stare. Let them blink. Let them assume you joined a pyramid scheme for emotions. The truth is simple. You learned a language that saved your life. A language built from rock-bottom wisdom, bad coffee, and forty adults bonding over thirty nights of chicken.

If the outside world does not understand your *Recovery-ese*, that is fine. You are not trying to be relatable. You are trying to stay alive.

So keep your slogans. Keep your serenity. Keep confusing civilians. Because if someone cannot handle your growth, your peace, or your rehab vocabulary, then congratulations. You just met someone who has never survived a small group with a counselor named *Jim*.

And honestly, that sounds like a them problem.

Recovery-ese to Civilian Translation Guide:

1- *"One Day at a Time"*
   Translation: *"If I think past bedtime, I'll end up in Vegas with a face tattoo."*

2- *"Let Go and Let God"*
   Translation: *"I'm done controlling this. God, Universe, Houseplant—whoever's on shift can have it."*

3- *"Progress, Not Perfection"*
   Translation: *"I didn't relapse. I did eat an entire cheesecake. We take those wins."*

4- *"HALT (Hungry, Angry, Lonely, Tired)"*
   Translation: *"You're not having an existential crisis, you just need a sandwich and a nap."*

5- *"Fake It 'Til You Make It"*
   Translation: *"Pretend you're a functioning adult until you accidentally become one."*

6- *"Nothing Changes If Nothing Changes"*
   Translation: *"Stop expecting miracles while still texting Chad at 3 a.m."*

7- *"Keep Coming Back"*
   Translation: *"Yes, it's boring. Yes, it's awkward. No, you don't graduate. Sorry, champ."*

8- *"It Works If You Work It"*
   Translation: *"This program is not Amazon Prime. Miracles aren't coming in two business days."*

9- *"Feelings Aren't Facts"*
   Translation: *"Yes, you're sad. No, Adele didn't write that song about you. Calm down, Linda."*

10- *"Stay in Your Lane"*
   Translation: *"Your lane has potholes, expired tags, and no insurance. Worry about that."*

20

Celebrate The Boring Day (Because "Nothing Happened" Is Actually A Win)

Nobody tells you this in rehab, but one day you wake up sober and life gets so boring you start wondering if you somehow died in your sleep and this is purgatory. You open your eyes and think, "*Hold up. This is it? This is Tuesday?*" Because in addiction, even your bad days had a plot twist. You were fighting somebody, crying over somebody, running from somebody, or doing something illegal with someone named *Dusty*. But now you wake up in your bed, in your house, with your face still on straight, and you think, "*Dang. Nothing is even on fire.*" No neck tattoo that says *FRITOS*. No mysterious bite mark shaped like the state of *Ohio*. No new roommate named *Rooster* living in your shed. No police radio crackling with, "*Yeah, we found her. The neighbors caught her on the Ring cam again stealing Amazon packages.*" No *Frankie Fentanyl* pulling up in his *Neon* saying, "*Hop in bro, we are hitting three counties today.*" No voicemail from a man named *Snakebite* asking if you still want the fireworks. No shoes missing. No memory missing. Just a quiet day. And you sit there going, "*This feels suspicious.*"

You spent so long chasing highs, surviving lows, and mistaking adrenaline for aliveness that calm feels foreign. You start pacing your clean kitchen thinking, "*Shouldn't I be saving someone? Crying? Losing a shoe?*" No. You should be sitting your miracle down and enjoying that big boy bowl of *Cap'n Crunch* before it sandpapers the roof of your mouth.

When you have lived in crisis long enough, you can mistake peace for emptiness. But boredom is not empty. It is spacious. It is room for your life to grow. The boring days are the ones you used to pray for. You begged the universe for one normal day. Now you have one and you are acting like it needs seasoning. Normal is the flavor. Taste it. For so long, stimulation was your anesthesia. Noise kept you numb. Stillness felt dangerous. Silence felt suspicious. Peace felt like the moment in a horror movie right before something jumps out and ruins your whole existence. So when nothing is happening, your brain panics because it does not know what safety feels like yet.

But boredom is proof your life is no longer on fire. Boring means stability. Boring means predictability. Boring means your worst problem today is running out of coffee, not running out of hope. And if you are not careful, you will start protecting your boring days like treasure. Because once you have lived through chaos that steals your peace, you realize boring is not punishment. It is the gift you fought for. You need consistency. You need calm. You need mornings that do not require apologies. You do not need fireworks. Shoutout to *Snakebite*.

Master the boring day. Honor it. Cherish it. Protect it. So the next time someone asks, "*How was your day?*" and all you can say is, "*Eh, nothing happened*," just smile. Because nothing happening used to be the dream. In recovery, boring is not the absence of excitement. It is the presence of *peace*.

10 Signs You're Having a Glorious, Boring Recovery Day:

1- The most adrenaline you felt today was when your Amazon package said "*out for delivery.*"

2- You got excited about a new sponge for the kitchen. Like, genuinely excited. *(You even showed your daughter. She didn't care.)*

3- You checked your mail and it wasn't a warrant, just *Bed Bath & Beyond* coupons.

4- You woke up fully clothed, in your own bed, with both shoes accounted for.

5- You scrolled through your texts from last night and didn't have to send a single "*ignore that, I was hacked*" message.

6 – You lit a candle for *"ambiance"* instead of to cover up bad decisions.

7 – You actually read the terms & conditions before clicking *"I agree." (Okay, skimmed. Still counts.)*

8 – The only *"mystery bruises"* now are from bumping into your coffee table, not from fights or *"stairs you didn't know existed."* (*Furniture: 1, you: 0.)*

9 – You didn't have to ask, *"Hey... do you remember what I did last night?"* Because you do—and it was the dishes.

10 – Your pee is so clear you debate posting it on *Instagram.* debate posting it on *Instagram. (#ClearFlex#SmartWaterWho)*

21

Tiny Victories Count—Even If It's Just Showering

People love to act like recovery is built on grand achievements. They talk about their thirty days sober like they just saved a dolphin from a fishing net. They smile like someone is about to lower confetti from the ceiling and cue a balloon drop. I love it for them, but that is not the truth. Recovery is not built in those big, dramatic, public moments. The real rebuilding does not happen when someone hands you a chip. It happens in the tiny, unglamorous moments long before anyone claps for you. It happens at home, alone, when you do not look anything like the inspirational quote you posted on *Pinterest* in 2019. Tiny victories are where everything actually shifts.

These are the moments that seem ridiculous from the outside but feel heroic from the inside. You brush your hair even though it is giving emotional cactus. You take a shower while negotiating with your own body, saying, *"Listen, I will wash my hair next Thursday. Today we just run the water and pretend."* You finally pick up that nightstand fork before it earns legal residency. You hear someone say something irritating, and instead of responding like you are auditioning for a reality show, you take a breath and walk away. Those tiny choices rebuild you quietly, stubbornly, one unsexy miracle at a time. Sometimes it just looks like an afternoon when you finally throw away a cereal box that has been empty since Easter. Every small choice is like whispering encouragement to yourself. Your brain loves that. Your brain responds like a proud parent at a kindergarten graduation, cheering for the absolute tiniest achievement.

Tiny victories matter because they prove to yourself that change is possible. Every small choice becomes a little note you leave yourself that says, *"Hey. You are still in the game."* People who have never lived in chaos will not understand why these things matter. They will see you celebrating making your bed and ask, *"Why is that such a big deal?"* That is when you turn slowly, lock eyes with them, and say, *"Because that bed almost killed me, Diane."* Some people need context. You do not owe *Diane* an explanation.

Tiny victories do not need applause. They do not need the internet. They do not need confetti. But try explaining that to the *Facebook* flaunters who post their five year sobriety update like they are announcing a presidential campaign. They include fourteen emojis, a *Canva* graphic of a dove rising out of a burning bush, and four hashtags: *#grateful #blessed #sober #grace.* *"All glory to God, five years sober today."* Their captions always read like they are trying to convince the internet, their ex, three cousins, and the universe itself that they are finally stable enough for a *Costco* membership again. Bless them. I truly wish them well. But let us be honest. Why is *Jennifer* from sixth grade the target audience for this announcement? What exactly do you expect her to do? Send you a certificate? Call *CNN*? Print your post and stick it on her refrigerator? You do not need fifty likes from people you would not loan five dollars to.

If you really want to make a difference, tell the man detoxing behind the gas station. Tell the woman sitting on the corner who smells like vodka and heartbreak. Tell the guy behind the grocery store who thinks hope is not meant for him. They need your story, not *Debbie* still selling *Scentsy Thompson* from ninth grade science class. You do not announce change. You live it. You do not post it. You prove it. You do not type paragraphs about how transformed you are. You let your life become so steady and so real that people feel it without you saying a word. Real transformation does not show up on *Facebook*. It shows up in how you move, how you breathe, how you do not clap back like you used to. Transformation does not need glitter. It leaves evidence.

This is why tiny victories matter. Your brain loves tiny wins. Your brain lights up like a toddler who just figured out high fives. You drink water and your organs cheer like they just got approved for low income housing. You take out the trash and your apartment reacts like you renovated it. You answer one text and suddenly feel emotionally qualified to run a small nonprofit. You put your shoes in the actual place they belong and suddenly your dead grandmother is whispering, *"Look at you acting like somebody."* These little wins stack. They build consistency. They build trust. They build you. And yes, some of them will look laughably small. But when you have lived in chaos, the basics become sacred.

If today you stayed alive, stayed present, hydrated yourself, held your tongue, made your bed, or simply existed without spiraling into a portal, you won. That counts. Nothing glamorous. Everything essential. So if you took even one small step toward healing today, even if no one noticed, no one clapped, and *Jennifer* from sixth grade did not hit like, that step was real. That step meant something. And that tiny little miracle might be the moment your whole life starts changing. And it is absolutely enough.

10 Tiny Rehab Wins That Deserve a Standing Ovation:

1- Keeping your cool when someone says, *"I know EXACTLY how you feel"* after knowing you for 4 hours.

2- Saying something halfway deep in group and hearing a couple *"mmm's"* like you just preached a sermon.

3- Catching a staff member break character and laugh at something inappropriate in group. Immortalized victory.

4- It's fried chicken night in the cafeteria and suddenly everyone believes in salvation again.

5- Room searches skip your room today. Your contraband *Lay's* live another day.

6- Seeing someone else fight with staff while you sit back with popcorn energy like, *"Not my circus."*

7- Group leader asks, *"Who wants to share first?"* and someone else sacrifices themselves like a true hero.

8- Movie night and nobody argues — it's *Step Brothers* unanimous.

9- The night shift nurse hands you m*elatonin* without the side-eye judgment look. Feels like respect.

10- You get assigned the counselor who swears sometimes — *instant credibility.*

22

Your Bed Knows Too Much

You cannot heal in the same environment that made you sick. That is not a self-help quote. That is physics and also common sense. You cannot take your same old life, slap a scented candle on it, and call it healing. Your environment becomes your accomplice. The walls know too much. The couch has witnessed things. Your bed could testify against you in court. Trying to heal there is like trying to lose weight inside a *Krispy Kreme*. The math is not mathing.

If the house you lived in was full of mold, you would not sit on the couch and manifest better lungs. You would leave. Immediately. Preferably wearing shoes. Your old environment was not only familiar. It was a problem. Yet we fight to stay. We defend our own doom. Humans cling to what they know. We would rather die in a groove we carved than live in a space we have never seen. But healing requires a relocation, even if you never pack a suitcase.

Rehab gives you distance. You start to realize this new place does not have ghosts. It has no memories, no triggers, and no spiritual potholes waiting to swallow you whole. It is only a building full of other feral adults trying not to ruin their lives in the same ways they did last season. For the first time in forever, your nervous system whispers that it can rest here. Nobody is trying to destroy you. It is just you, surrounded by people who are just as confused, trying not to become the person they used to be.

Back in your old life, Friday at seven in the evening meant sitting in the parking lot of the liquor store giving yourself a pep talk about how you deserved it. In treatment, Friday at seven means sitting in a coping skills lecture eating pretzels that taste like they lost custody of their salt. One version keeps you alive. The other keeps you crying in your car while listening to sad playlists.

Sometimes healing means changing your habitat and some-times healing means changing the humans in it. Healing will threaten anyone who benefited from your dysfunction. Your sobriety will confuse anyone who liked you better when you were messy. Your peace will upset anyone who relied on your chaos. Some people will cheer for your healing. Others will behave as if you personally attacked their character development. Your decision to change your life will offend those who benefited from you staying sick.

Comfort should never be mistaken for safety. Sometimes comfort is the trap. Sometimes comfort is the poison. Comfortable can kill you faster than cocaine. When you gain distance, your old world begins to look dusty. Your favorite bar no longer feels like home. It looks sad. Your *"fun friend"* begins to resemble someone trapped in a loop they cannot see. Your old apartment suddenly looks like the *"before"* picture in a documentary about dysfunction.

Eventually, you might return, but you will walk in like a landlord doing an inspection. Even the smallest changes matter. You will move furniture. You will clean your closets. You will sage the old memories. You will open windows as if releasing trapped spirits. You are not moving back as the old tenant. You are returning as the owner. The environment did not change. You did. Every new choice becomes a tiny billboard that says you are under new management.

Your brain will protest. Brains hate change. Brains also made most of your bad decisions, so they should not be allowed to vote right now. Your brain misses the sickness because the sickness was predictable. Healing is unpredictable. Healing is scary. *Dying is scary too.* Healing is not about erasing your past. It is about refusing to reenact it. Changing your environment is not losing yourself. It is losing the version of you who almost did not make it.

If the environment that broke you could heal you, you would already be healed. Your old environment will not heal you. Getting out will. Changing your scenery is not about changing the view. It is about finally being able to see yourself, the version of you who survives, the version of you who chooses differently, the version of you who no longer runs into a burning house because you finally believe you deserve more than ashes.

Wake up. Walk out. Stop apologizing for burning down a chapter that was trying to bury you. If you stay where you got sick, you will stay sick. If you leave, you might meet the person you were born to become.

10 Reasons You Can't Heal in the Same Place You Got Sick:

1- Neighbors never forget. You think you're walking out proud and sober. They're peeking through blinds like, *"Isn't that the chick who stole Amazon packages?"*

2- Your old bathroom mirror is a hater. You stand there brushing your teeth, and it's like, *"Girl, I've seen things."*

3- Your couch is a crime scene. You think it's "cozy." The stains say, *"We saw you destroy yourself here."* Burn it.

4- Because the ghosts never shut up. Every song, every smell, every stupid corner of that place screams, *"Remember when you ruined everything here?"*

5- Because the carpet is a narc. No matter how many times you vacuum, it knows what went down there.

6- Because habits are squatters. They don't leave just because you changed your mind. You've gotta evict them with new places and new routines, or they'll trash the joint again.

7- Because comfort zones are coffins. They feel safe because you already know the shape. Problem is, they're also where you were slowly dying.

8- Because you're not stronger than gravity. You can't stand on the same slippery floor and expect not to fall again. Physics doesn't give a damn about your affirmations.

9- Because you don't recover in the crime scene. You don't fix a marriage in the hotel where you cheated. Same logic. Get out.

10- Because hell has home-field advantage. You can't win a war in the enemy's living room. Same place, same poison, same ending. *Period.*

23

One Day You'll Miss Batman Checking On You In The Bathroom

Nobody shows up to rehab thinking, *"You know what, one day I am going to miss this joint."* Walking in for the first time feels like wandering into the wrong funeral. Everyone looks at you. You look at them. Nobody knows what is happening. You walk inside like a stray dog that got tricked with a piece of cheese. Someone hands you papers. Someone else hands you rules. Nobody tells you where to stand. Nobody tells you where to put your suitcase. You stand there like a confused *Sims* character waiting for your player to click something. Someone asks if you have had thoughts of harming yourself or others or the microwave. You think, *"This is hell."*

The building looks like a middle school that failed its inspection. Someone hands you a pen that barely works. Someone else tells you to take your socks off and show the bottom of your feet while another person asks you to squat and cough. *Nothing about this feels legal.* You stand there holding your belt and shoelaces, questioning every decision that led you here. They take your phone. They take your freedom. They take your confidence that you will ever shower in peace again. Then intake begins. A nurse asks about your childhood, your relationships, your drug of choice, and what your stool has looked like for the past two weeks without blinking. You think, "*I do not even tell my doctor this. Who are you?*" Your first walk around the unit feels like an identity crisis. Do I look like I belong? Does everyone know I have no idea what I am doing? Why is a dude named *Spider* staring at me? Why did they take my goose-down pillow? Why does everyone look like they should not legally be around scissors?

At first you resist. You are a raccoon in a cage. Angry. Hissing. Ready to bite. You are convinced that the second those doors open you will sprint out like *Forrest Gump* with an ankle monitor. Straight to your own bed, a twenty-piece *McNugget*, maybe *Starbucks* if you are trying to be classy. You swear you will never miss this place. Not even a little. But rehab is sneaky. Rehab is the weird uncle who shows up uninvited and somehow becomes your favorite relative. You hate it. You tolerate it. Then twenty-two days in you are laughing so loudly the night staff threatens to separate the group. When it is time for discharge, people hug you. Someone slips you their number even though they are not supposed to. Someone signs your *Big Book* like a high school yearbook. Somebody cries. Somebody gives you a note. Somebody steals your shampoo. All normal stuff.

The mean counselor pats you on the back and says, *"You did good,"* and your chest cracks open because you have not heard praise like that since your driver's test. You walk out. The sunlight hits you. The world is loud. Your brain is louder. Everything feels bright and too open. You realize you are walking away from the only place where you did not have to pretend. The place where your broken parts did not scare anyone. The place where people celebrated you for brushing your hair. You go home. You open your fridge and stare at it like it is a portal to loneliness. It is just you and your thoughts now. Lonely. Empty. Quiet. Too quiet. No knock asking if you are coming to group. No laughter in the hallway. No chaos to distract you. Nobody asking how you slept. Nobody congratulating you for resisting a craving. No weird roommate asking if you want to split a pudding cup. Sometimes the silence feels louder than addiction ever did. It does not whisper. It echoes.

And then the truth hits you. The truth nobody warns you about. You miss it. You miss the structure. Breakfast, group, lunch, group, dinner, group. A day so stitched together it felt like your life had finally hired a seamstress. You miss how, if you sat in the bathroom longer than the *Lord's Prayer*, a tech appeared like *Batman*. *"Hey bud, you alive? You journaling? You pooping? You crying while pooping? Give us a thumbs-up."* In the real world you can be missing for weeks and your family thinks you took a nap. You could be face down in your driveway and your neighbors would assume you were doing yoga.

Inside those walls, you were never invisible. You do not miss the six a.m. vitals. You do not miss staff creeping into rooms

125

at three in the morning with flashlights like they were filming *Ghost Hunters: Rehab Edition.* You do not miss sharing a bathroom with a man who smelled like microwaved onions inside a sock. But you miss the small, stupid, sacred moments that held you together. The roommate chaos. Someone stealing your pillow. Someone hoarding apples like they are preparing for famine or secretly baking pies. One guy snoring so loudly the walls vibrate. Someone walking into group wrapped in a blanket like a cult leader. A dude with two days sober announcing he is writing a book. A man trying to flush a pair of socks.

And the smoke breaks. Thirty people in mismatched pajama pants sharing one grill lighter that somehow holds more emotional authority than the presidency. Smoke break is church. Smoke break is therapy. Smoke break is the courts, the streets, the barbershop, the confessional. Someone new in detox is shaking so hard their cigarette spells out Morse code for "*help.*" People laughing. People crying. People trauma-dumping. People flirting even though nobody has showered. You start learning people's stories. Hearing things that rearrange your insides. Caring without realizing it. Someone shares a story so wild it resets the group's serotonin. Someone else says she does not even like cigarettes, she just likes standing in a circle. You cannot recreate that in the real world. If you stand outside a gas station crying and smoking, people *call the police.*

Then comes the honesty. Rehab honesty is not polite honesty. It is raw truth spoken by people who have run out of lies. A man in detox admitting he still wants to use even though he lost custody of his kids. A girl whispering that she does not think she is worth saving. A counselor looking straight through you saying, *"You can keep lying, but it is not going to keep you alive."* People say they hate themselves. People say they do not know how to survive without chaos. Someone admits she does not know how to stay alive when she is alone. Your heart feels too big for your ribcage. People cry because they miss their dog. Because they miss tater tots. Because their ex tried to run them over in a *Walmart* parking lot and they still miss him. Nobody pretends. Nobody angles for the best lighting. Even the eye rolls are honest. Rehab honesty stings, but it saves.

And what you never expect to miss is the connection. Addiction shrinks your life until it is just you and the substance, your own toxic two-person cult. A fake smile for your mom. A *"you up"* text to your dealer. Silence everywhere else. Then rehab throws you into a room with forty broken strangers and suddenly you are having real conversations. *"I do not want to live today."* And nobody panics because everyone has stood in that same dark hallway. For the first time in forever, you feel seen. The relief is unreal. Someone shares a story and you think, *"Thank God, I am not the only idiot who did that."* Connection shows up everywhere. In the TV wars when someone dares change the channel from *Judge Judy*. In the med line where everyone waits like it is the DMV. In the card games that almost become fistfights. In the sarcastic applause for the one guy who actually arrives to group on time. You miss the people who sat beside you in the dark without trying to fix you. You miss the proof that you mattered. You miss the place where you did not have to be perfect to deserve love. You miss being seen in all your mess. You miss the strange rehab version of affection made entirely of sarcasm and shared trauma.

Rehab was chaos. Rehab was uncomfortable. Rehab was embarrassing on a cellular level. Instant oatmeal. Borrowed blankets. Mandatory icebreakers that felt like punishment. Rehab made you furious. Rehab made you vulnerable. Rehab stole your dignity and then returned it one piece at a time. But it was the first place you stopped pretending. The first place you let your guard down. The first place you were seen without having to earn it. The first place where your pain was not a burden. The first place where you felt less alone in your worst moments. You did not just survive. You witnessed other people survive. And when you have been invisible for years, being witnessed feels like resurrection. It was the place where your existence mattered. Your breath mattered. Your tiny victories mattered. Your honesty was not too heavy. Your humanity was not too much. People knew your trauma before they knew your last name. They knew your bedtime anxiety before they knew where you worked. They knew your relapse triggers before they knew if you had siblings.

It was the only place your where your tears were not embarrassing. Where your story was never too much. You miss the only place in your life where you could fall apart and be met with, "*Aight man, get up slow. We are not letting you go out like that.*" It is love. But feral love. Wild animal love. "*I found you in a ditch and adopted you*" love. People do not know how to love normally, so they love in rehab dialect. "*You look like complete and utter sh**. Come sit with me.*" Messy love. Inconvenient love. Real love.

That is when you realize the connection was not extra. It was the point. Everything else was background noise. What kept you alive was people dragging you through the mess even when they had nothing left. And the proof stays burned in your memory. Rehab is the only place on earth where someone can storm out yelling, "*I am done. I am leaving. I am going AMA and nobody can stop me,*" kick open a door, march out like they are escaping federal custody, and then reappear forty-seven minutes later standing in line for meds asking if anyone knows what is for dinner. Everyone pretends to be annoyed and roll their eyes, but the truth is simple. They are relieved. Because it means one more person stayed alive.

10 Things You'll Weirdly Miss About Rehab:

1- That one guy who thinks he's everyone's sponsor. He's got three weeks more clean time than you and suddenly he's *Confucius* with a nicotine patch.

2- You start craving smoke pit gossip like it was oxygen. Your coworkers' stories don't hit the same. Now, you stand on your porch smoking alone. And realize without rehab, it's not "*bonding,*" it's just SAD.

3- People inventing workouts with broken furniture. Who needs a gym when you've got a busted chair and a half-flat basketball?

4- The hookup conspiracies staff clocked instantly. You thought you were sneaky? Nah. Staff knew who was crushing on who before you did — like middle school teachers at a dance.

5- The 7 a.m. uppity walking crew that treated doing laps around the parking lot like it was the *Tour de France*.

6- Spades games that ended in death threats. Because nothing kills serenity like your partner cutting hearts when you still had spades in your hand.

7- You realize no one's drug-testing you anymore. And that's somehow scarier than when they did.

8- You stare at your calendar and miss the dry erase board... because *"Doctor appointment"* doesn't hit the same as *"Feelings Group @ 3."*

9- Group shares that went from deep trauma to *"and that's why I don't f*** with Taco Bell anymore."*

10- That weird, messed-up little family you swore you hated... but still miss, because only they know exactly how insane and hilarious it all was.

24

Emotional Terms & Conditions (I Never Agreed To)

Nobody gets a tutorial for this. At birth they slap you, hand you a social security number, and release you into the wild like, *"Good luck, tiny creature. Hope you figure out taxes and heartbreak."* One minute you are learning how to hold your own head up and the next minute people expect you to understand emotions and insurance deductibles. That is the onboarding. Suddenly you are expected to understand relationships, laundry, medical bills, disappointment, joy, and grief. None of this is optional. Welcome to the contract.

Addiction, for a while, feels like a loophole. A little escape hatch where nothing is required of you except existing. Feelings get muted. Problems get delayed. Life gets put on silent mode like you are blocking a telemarketer. Substances were not just coping. They were your pause button on a life you did not yet have the tools to carry. So when someone in rehab smiles and says, *"You need to live life on life's terms,"* you look around like, *"Oh? With what resources? With what skill set? With what five-year emotional degree I never got?"* If you could live life on life's terms, I would not have shown a complete stranger the soles of my feet. But something starts to happen quietly, slowly, and accidentally. You start hearing again.

Addiction makes people deaf. Recovery turns the volume back up. Life did not suddenly get louder. You just stopped muting it. Recovery does not make life easier. It makes life make sense. It stops asking the world to change and starts teaching you how to not fall apart every time the wind blows sideways. It teaches you that feelings do not kill you. Honesty does not break you. Asking for help does not shrink you. Cravings pass. Silence is survivable. Being alive is strangely manageable once you stop treating every discomfort like divine punishment.

Life is not waiting for anyone to get their emotional self together. Life is not standing in the corner holding your purse whispering, *"Take your time, sweetie."* Life is already in the car laying on the horn. Life is emailing you. Life is calling you. Life is knocking on your bathroom door like, *"Hey babe, your kid just ate a crayon and the water bill is late."* But eventually your reactions change. Not all at once and not with fireworks, but they shift. A flat tire stops being a prophecy. A bad hour stops meaning a bad life. A craving stops meaning a relapse. You stop taking every inconvenience personally.

Life's terms do not mean believing the universe hates you. Life's terms mean understanding the universe is simply doing what it always does, *existing with or without your approval.* Life is not trying to destroy anyone. Life is trying to grow people up. Growth always applies pressure. Diamonds do not form under gentle encouragement. Neither do adults.

At some point the fight drains out and something steadier moves in. A version of you that does not crumble every time the afternoon shows up with an attitude. A version that can hold a life instead of hiding from it. A version that can survive discomfort without immediately searching for an exit sign. Recovery eventually hands you a new set of internal truths. You can feel something uncomfortable and live. You can tell the truth and keep your dignity. You can ask for help and still be fully grown. You can make it through a bad day without using. You can stop escaping your life and start inhabiting it.

Then one day you catch yourself handling something that would have taken you out emotionally, mentally, spiritually, and possibly physically. Instead of collapsing, you just breathe, adjust your ponytail, roll your eyes, and think, *"Okay life, drop the lesson. I will catch it. I may cuss, but I will catch it."* That is the moment you know you are different now. Life did not get easier. You got sturdier.

Suddenly you are not begging life to calm down. You are meeting life in the parking lot like, *"Say it with your chest then."* You are the adult now. A confused adult, sure, but an adult nonetheless. And slowly the perks begin showing up. A sunset that looks edited. A laugh that feels like medicine. A random afternoon where your brain thinks, *"I like being alive,"* and you almost fall over because that thought used to feel impossible.

That is when the chapter turns. That is when the mic drop lands. Life did not change. You did. You went from unraveling over small things to walking into chaos with the energy of someone who has survived their own chaos and therefore fears nothing while still remembering to take out the trash. You became someone who can do hard things annoyed, which is honestly the most adult place a person can live.

Living life on life's terms is not glamorous. It is not candles and bath bombs and perfectly aligned chakras. It is showing up. When it is heavy. When it is boring. When it is beautiful. When it is chaotic and unhinged and feels like the universe woke up in a mood. It is not perfection. It is presence. And one day you stop mid-task, look around, and think, "*Hold up. Who the heck am I right now?*" Because for the first time in your entire messy, brilliant existence, you are not waiting for life to stop being wild. You are simply becoming the version of yourself who can walk through that wildness without losing yourself.

Life's terms never changed. The player did. And the upgraded version of you. They do not play.

10 Life Terms Nobody Warned You About:

1- Cravings don't RSVP. They show up like your toxic ex at 2 a.m. — uninvited, loud, and full of bad ideas.

2- Other people's opinions are guaranteed. They'll talk

whether you relapse or run for president. **Might as well do you.**

3- Laughter is mandatory. Skip it, and you'll end up writing moody *Facebook* poems at 3 a.m.

4- Meetings are forever. Even when you're old, cranky, and smell like mothballs, someone will still be reading *How It Works* in a monotone voice.

5- Half your new coping skills are just kindergarten rules. Naps, coloring, using your words — congrats, you're basically five with bills.

6- Your romantic radar is broken AF. If they have a pulse and a court date, your brain screams *"Soulmate!"* Don't trust it.

7- Connection isn't optional. The opposite of addiction isn't *"lone wolf vibes"* — it's awkward hugs, messy group shares, and someone stealing your lighter.

8- Your pets don't trust you. That cat remembers when you forgot to feed her for two days. She's judging every move you make.

9- Apologies multiply like rabbits. You'll start apologizing for stuff people don't even remember. *"Sorry for stealing your eyeliner in 2009."* They're like, *"...what?"*

10- Life doesn't get easier. You just get funnier, pettier, and brutally honest — basically the person you always wished was

sitting next to you in group.

25

I Am Dramatic and Need Supervision (So Here's the Plan)

Relapse does not start with the substance. Relapse starts when your brain gets quiet. It is like having a toddler in the next room who suddenly stops making noise. You know in your soul either they are drawing on the dog or trying to baptize a sibling in the toilet. That quiet is not peace. That quiet is warning. Something is getting cut, colored on, or set on fire. When my brain went silent like that, I should have checked on myself.

For the longest time, I believed relapse was the moment I picked up. I thought the danger lived in the drink or the pill. But relapse always started earlier. It started in the loneliness I brushed off, the resentment I swallowed, the stress I minimized, and the feelings I refused to name. It started every time I said "*I'm fine*" when I was anything but. Relapse begins the moment you drift away from yourself.

That is why relapse planning exists. Not because someone thinks you are doomed. Not because they are sizing you up like, *"Yeah, this one is definitely gonna slip."* No. A relapse plan is admitting you are the kind of person who can go downhill quietly. You will not even hear yourself falling. You will not see the cliff. You will just suddenly be at the bottom like, *"Damn, who pushed me?"* Nobody. It was you. You just were not paying attention.

Relapse prevention is not strength. It is honesty. Honest enough to say you are lonely. Honest enough to admit you are overwhelmed. Honest enough to tell someone, *"If I do not talk to a person today, I am going to talk to the wrong thing."* Cravings do not start the party. Cravings are late to the party. Disconnection sends the invites, buys the snacks, and opens the door.

When I understood that, relapse planning stopped feeling like punishment and started feeling like protection. It is not a worksheet. It is a map. It is a map of your rhythms, your danger zones, your quiet moments, and the places you tend to abandon yourself. It shows you the whispers that come long before anything gets loud. It is basically *Google Maps* for your nervous system: *"In 300 feet, you will lie to yourself. Please turn right."*

Recovery is not about white-knuckling your way through life. Relapse prevention is not about willpower. Willpower is the friend who hypes you up and then disappears when the cops show up. Willpower lies. Awareness will not. Awareness, connection, and honesty will save you long before strength ever will.

Relapse usually has nothing to do with wanting to feel high. Most of the time, it is about not wanting to feel at all. It comes from overwhelm, loneliness, boredom that feels like static in your bones, and unresolved memories you tried to outrun. It comes from telling yourself you can "*handle it now,*" as if your addiction were a small, obedient house pet that finally learned manners.

The truth is simple. Learn yourself. Learn your early warnings. Learn the shift in your own mood before it snowballs. Learn the difference between "*I need rest*" and "*I need to disappear into a cornfield, where I end up doing shady things with some kids named Isaac and Malachai.*" When you know how you lose yourself, you also know how to find your way back.

A relapse plan is you saying, "*Look... I know myself. I am dramatic. I get overwhelmed. I spiral fast. I will do something dumb if I do not speak up.*" My relapse plan is not a rulebook. It is a promise. A promise that I will not abandon myself again. A promise to tell the truth sooner. A promise to stay connected even when it feels uncomfortable. A promise to choose the life I fought for over the lie that escape will save me.

You do not plan because you expect to relapse. You do not plan because you are weak. You plan because you are powerful. You plan because you know your life matters. You plan because you finally understand you are worth protecting.

139

10 Sample Relapse Prevention Plans for People Who Know Themselves Too Well:

1- Trigger: Someone offers me "*just one.*"
  Plan: Pretend they just offered me sushi from a gas station. Disgust. Immediate no.

2- Trigger: Thinking "*I've got this handled now.*"
  Plan: Run, don't walk, to a meeting—because clearly, I do not "*have this.*"

3- Trigger: "*Celebrating*" something small.
  Plan: Buy a sheet cake and get your name written on it in icing. Congratulations, you lived through *Tuesday.*

4- Trigger: Running into old using buddies.
  Plan: Smile, wave, and treat them like mall kiosk workers. "*No thanks, I don't want lotion or relapse today.*"

5- Trigger: Feeling like I "*deserve*" a break.
  Plan: Take a nap or a bubble bath. Not a "*vacation package*" straight back to county jail.

6- Trigger: Romanticizing the "*good old days.*"
  Plan: Rewatch the real highlight reel: searching the carpet on your hands and knees, panic *Googling "can vodka expire,"* and waking up in shoes that weren't yours.

7- Trigger: Sitting in silence too long.
  Plan: Narrate your life out loud like you're in *The Office.*

8- Trigger: Payday boredom.

Plan: Buy something ridiculously wholesome, like matching socks or a vacuum. Flex hard about it.

9- Trigger: Loneliness on a Saturday night.

Plan: Order too much takeout, pass out halfway through the movie, and call it *"self-care."*

10- Trigger: Someone says, *"Come on, live a little."*

Plan: Politely reply, *"I did. Almost died. Hard pass."*

26

Your Inner Child Does Not Want Closure. It Wants a Slip and Slide.

Closure is a scam. Closure is what people ask their ex for when they want to pretend they are emotionally mature, even though the real goal is to see whether the other person aged badly. Closure is a costume of healing. It is a polite exchange where two people sit across from each other pretending they are there to untangle the past, when the truth is that both are checking for signs of who lost the breakup.

Your inner child has no interest in any of that. Your inner child is not fragile. Your inner child is wild. They have been locked inside you for years. They have watched you overthink, over explain, over apologize, and over function your way through life. They have waited like a bored kid stuck in the backseat while you kept saying you were only running into the store for one minute. And here you are, in rehab, finally slowing down long enough for that kid to crawl out of the backseat holding a *Capri Sun* and a packet of fruit snacks. They look at you with the kind of authority that cannot be argued with and say, *"Quit bonding over trauma. Come play."*

You do not expect to listen. You certainly do not expect to obey. But something in you responds, something ancient, something innocent. So you run. You play. You, a fully grown adult with a long medical history and a brain that has been on high alert for years, suddenly find yourself sprinting across a courtyard because your inner child dared you to. Then it happens. You feel something that is not fear and not guilt and not shame. You feel joy. It arrives with the surprise and force of a badminton racket that came out of nowhere. It feels like the universe leaned down, whispered in your ear, and reminded you that you are supposed to be alive, not simply surviving.

Here is the part nobody tells you. The deepest healing you will experience in rehab will not happen in group. It will not show up in that beige room where a man named *Lewis* tries to explain cognitive distortions while wrestling a granola bar he appears to be losing to. It will not happen during worksheets filled with terms like *rumination* and *maladaptive*, which sound like illnesses you would catch on a cruise ship. Real healing sneaks up on you in the stupidest moment imaginable. It happens at two thirty on a random Monday when staff announces, *"Alright guys, free time."*

Free time in rehab is wild. It is recess for adults who have been emotionally hit by a bus. Everyone shuffles outside pretending they are too cool to play. Blank faces. Arms folded. Acting like

143

they are waiting for a hostage negotiation instead of sunlight. You walk out with your arms crossed and think, *"I do not play. I am grown. I have seen things."* Then someone rolls out a basketball that looks one bounce away from hospice. You pick it up without thinking. It is heavy in all the wrong places and gasping for air. The goal is leaning so far to the side it looks like it needs its own physical therapy appointment. You take a shot anyway. It misses by an entire ZIP code.

Someone yells *"Airball."* It sounds like this is the moment he has been waiting his whole life to announce. And for the first time in a long time, you laugh. Not a polite laugh. Not a careful one. A real laugh that comes from your lungs and your spine and maybe even a forgotten place near your soul. A laugh that shakes something loose inside you. Around you, other people begin to laugh too. These are people with backstories that would break most humans. People with losses and charges and regrets and wounds that never healed right. People who have cried into pillows and steering wheels and their own hands. And now they are laughing like the world never took anything from them at all.

Cornhole is happening nearby with beanbags that look like they are leaking ancient birdseed. Inside, a heated argument is happening about whether a ping pong serve was legal. The Spades table is a battleground. You have not known true betrayal until you have watched someone slam the Queen of Spades, shake the table, and shout, *"You cut me. You actually cut me."* *Spider* is insisting on a house rule that he claims came from his cousin in 1997. No one questions him. We follow it like scripture. Someone else threatens to flip the whole table.

There is no prize, no money, no trophy, nothing at stake except pride and unresolved childhood wounds.

It is absolute chaos. Plastic coated joy. Holy noise. And it is the healthiest thing you have felt in years. By the time most of us reach rehab, joy feels complicated. Fun feels foreign. Laughter is something we ration like groceries. Life has been heavy for so long that doing something simply because it feels good does not even register as an option. So when someone says, *"Come outside,"* you look around like, *"Is this a trick. Where is the processing worksheet. Who is about to ask about my childhood."*

But something shifts. Slowly at first. Then all at once. For the first time in years, your nervous system unclenches. Your guard lowers. Your soul stretches in ways it forgot it could. Something inside you wakes up. You realize that you did not forget how to play. You only forgot how good it feels to be *alive*.

Let me tell you a story. One day I was asked to lead a nursing group. People walked in expecting a lecture about liver damage or sleep hygiene or why combining meth with *Monster Energy* drinks is a lifestyle choice the human body cannot endorse. They sat down with arms crossed. Someone asked what the topic was. Without thinking I said, *"Music Bingo."* They stared at me like I had confessed to malpractice. *"This is a nursing group,"* one patient said. I smiled. *"Exactly. And today we treat the nervous system with Marvin Gaye."* A man in the back who always looked annoyed with oxygen said, *"We already had rec therapy today."* In my head I thought, *"And your point is?,"* but out loud I said, *"Fun is a non pharmacological intervention.*

Please take your complaints to the Joint Commission."

The room exploded with laughter. Except him. He blinked at me like joy was something he had never experienced personally. Then there was a patient I will call *Joe. Joe* was older, quiet, a veteran. He used a cane. He asked for *Tylenol* every day. He never smiled. He never spoke. He carried trauma in his posture and pain in every slow step. We started playing. Different songs. Different decades. A track from the seventies started and before the first few seconds finished, *Joe* stood up. Not slowly. Not cautiously. He simply rose. He straightened his back. He let his cane *fall*. And then he danced.

This man, who moved like life had dragged him behind it for decades, suddenly began shuffling and grooving like his bones remembered something his mind had forgotten. The room froze. One patient yelled, *"Joe, we thought you could not walk."* *Joe* shouted back, *"This is my jam, baby."* The room erupted. People jumped up and joined him. Laughter filled the space. A chant broke out. *"Go Joe, go Joe, go Joe."* *Joe* was swaying and snapping his fingers. He had a grin as wide as his face. Trauma loosened its grip. Joy entered the room. Something sacred happened. When the song ended, Joe sat back down. After group, he picked up his cane and walked out. Before he left, he looked back at me while smiling and said quietly, *"Ma'am, I needed that."*

The truth settled deep inside all of us. Closure does not heal the soul. Joy does. Play does. Connection does. Your inner child does not want a detailed discussion about the past. They do not want a final conversation or a tidy explanation. They want movement. They want freedom. They want sunlight on your face and the feeling of running too fast. They want a slip and slide across the lawn with water spraying everywhere and grass sticking to your shins.

Your trauma wants you silent. Your shame wants you still. Your guilt wants you small. Your inner child wants you alive. They want you laughing so loudly that a counselor pokes their head in and says, "*Guys, let us keep it down,*" like an annoyed landlord. They want you remembering who you were before the world asked you to toughen up. They want you waking up the parts of yourself that stopped believing life could be fun.

You cannot heal the hurting parts of yourself until you reconnect with the parts that know how to live. So if you hear your inner child calling, do not analyze it. Do not put it on a list. Do not wait for the right moment. Just go. Run. Laugh. Play. Slide across the metaphorical slip and slide of your own life like your soul depends on it. *Because it probably does.*

10 Signs You're Finding Your Inner Child Again:

1- The rec therapist pulls out the karaoke machine and you belt "*Don't Stop Believin'*" like that small-town girl is *YOU* and rehab is your *Madison Square Garden.*

2- You volunteer to hand out pencils and it feels like you have been elected president of something important.

3- You organize a nature walk even though it is just loops around a pond that looks like it needs antibiotics.

4- You find yourself genuinely invested in a puzzle with three missing pieces like you are solving a cold case.

5- You try to stay mature during meditation but start giggling because someone's stomach growled like a demon trying to escape generational poverty.

6- You feel a wild, feral thrill when someone yells *"FREE TIME,"* the same thrill you used to get when the teacher said *"recess"* before life introduced you to felony charges and co-payments.

7- You ask the cafeteria staff if they have *"seconds"* with the desperate sincerity of a child in elementary school hoping the lunch lady who smokes menthols behind the dumpster is in a good mood today.

8- You sneak a juice cup out of the cafeteria and drink it behind a tree like you are doing something illegal. It is apple juice. You feel powerful.

9- You are hyped for the Sunday ping-pong tournament *Big Country* organized even though the table leans, the paddles peel, and the ball has seen more trauma than half the unit, and you scream *"LET'S GO!"* after every point like you are on *ESPN*.

10- Out of nowhere, something tiny flickers in your chest, a soft little spark whispering, *"Hey... maybe life gets good again."*

27

I Wasn't Crazy, I Was Just High

I did not expect the first big truth of sobriety to hit me in my own living room, but it did. It landed so cleanly I had to laugh. It turns out I was not the crazy one. I was just high. I had no idea how much that simple fact would change the way I saw everything around me.

Leaving rehab gives you a glow that should probably come with a warning label. You walk out feeling hopeful, grounded, and spiritually moisturized, like a plant that finally got real sunlight. You picture yourself walking back into your home with soft lamps glowing, gentle hugs waiting, maybe even a proud tear rolling down someone's cheek. You imagine someone whispering how strong you are. Maybe there is a rainbow. Maybe *Morgan Freeman* narrates the whole thing.

Yeah. *No.*

When I walked in with my 30-day chip held high like it was an award, I delivered the most heartfelt amends speech of my life. My kid listened, nodded once, and said, *"Cool. Can you give me a ride to Jason's house?"* That was my entire welcome-home parade. No applause. No music swelling in the background. Just me, my chip, and someone needing a ride.

It took five minutes of standing there to understand that nothing had changed except me. My mother was already yelling about something from 1997 and weaponizing guilt the way some people collect coupons. My sister was lying about something nobody asked her. My kids rolled their eyes like they were trying to look behind themselves. My cousin was in the corner yelling at the dog in Spanish, and the dog still did not speak Spanish. It felt like stepping into a sitcom rerun everyone else had memorized while I was watching it sober for the very first time.

I sat down in the middle of a full-blown argument about a missing phone charger and felt clarity settle over me. These people had not changed at all. Not an inch. They were wearing the exact same emotional outfits they had on when I left. Rehab was safe and predictable. Home felt like it had been produced by the same people who make *The Hunger Games*.

I had spent thirty days learning to regulate my nervous system. I walked back into a family that did not regulate anything. They were marinated, soaked all the way through in generational trauma, caffeine, gossip, and resentments old enough to vote. I came in thinking quietly that I had healed. They greeted me with a brand-new list of things I had apparently forgotten to feel guilty about.

That was the moment I saw what sobriety had been trying to show me. I was never the only dysfunctional one. I was simply the only obvious one. My addiction did not make me the problem. It made my pain loud enough for everyone to see.

Their chaos hid behind polite casseroles, perfectly timed sighs, shopping bags, and silent avoidance. Mine refused to stay quiet. Their issues lived underground like an emotional septic tank. Mine spilled onto the sidewalk where everyone could trip right over it. Before recovery, I believed I was the unstable one. Now I could finally see the truth. *We were all unstable.* I was just the only one whose symptoms did not know how to whisper.

Suddenly, everything sounded different. Every sigh, every interruption, every dramatic retelling felt like a neon sign flashing the words untreated something. They did not apologize. They did not communicate. They did not regulate emotions. They did not respect boundaries. They did not self-reflect. They did not do any of the work I had just crawled through. Sobriety did not just clear my head. It cleared the fog that had been protecting them.

For a split second, I pictured gathering everyone in the living room for a class called *Emotional Regulation*. I saw myself with a whiteboard, diagrams, maybe even stickers. Then I remembered exactly who I was dealing with. If I tried that, someone would start yelling, someone else would cry, someone would storm outside to smoke, and my sister would loudly announce that I went to rehab once and now I think I am *Dr. Phil* with bangs.

So instead of teaching a class that nobody enrolled in, I sat quietly and breathed the way my counselor taught me. *Aunt Linda* grabbed my arm, shook it like a vending machine, and demanded to know why I was being so quiet. I told her I was regulating my nervous system. She blinked and told me to stop because I was freaking her out. And that was when I understood it fully. I was not returning to a new home. I was returning as a new person to an old one.

There comes a point in early recovery where you stop trying to upgrade everyone else and start protecting the work you have done inside yourself. You cannot police everyone's coping skills. You cannot walk around acting like the sobriety sheriff. You cannot sponsor an entire family that treats boundaries like disrespect. Recovery is not about turning the people you love into better versions of themselves. Recovery is about not losing yourself around the versions they still are.

The truth is simple. If they were emotionally capable of changing, they would have done it already. My job now is to hold on to the clarity, the boundaries, and the self-respect I earned, even if cabinets are slamming in the background. Sobriety taught me how to feel again. Coming home taught me how to stay steady while everyone else continued feeling however they felt.

I used to think peace meant changing the room. Now I know real peace is keeping mine no matter what room I walk into.

You Get a Step! You Get a Step! Everybody Gets a Step!
You can't unsee it now — and start assigning steps:

Step 1 — Your son *Elijah*
Powerless over *"forgetting"* trash day... *Again. And again.*

Step 2 — Your sister *Elizabeth*
Her Higher Power is vaping and sighing dramatically while reminding everyone, *"I do EVERYTHING for this family."*

Step 3 — Your mom *Karen*
Needs to turn her will (and her *Facebook* password) over... *To literally anyone.*

Step 4 — Your daughter *Nicole*
Her moral inventory should start with every time she said, *"No offense, but..."* *-right before being offensive.*

Step 5 — Your ex-husband *Drew*
Needs to admit to *God*, himself, and everybody else that *"going out for milk"* in 2004 was never about milk... *I knew, I always knew.*

Step 6 — Your best friend *Angela*
Needs to become entirely ready to dump him... *Instead of rewatching his Snapstory 47 times to see if that couch in the background belongs to another woman.*

Step 7 — *You*
Asked *God* to remove your shortcomings... *Then immediately*

argued to keep sarcasm, pettiness, and caffeine addiction.

Step 8 — Your brother *Davis*
Needs to make a list of all the people he's ticked off this week... *Yes, it's longer than last week's.*

Step 9 — Uncle *Ron*
Still owes you $40 from 1998... *Time to make amends, champ.*

Step 10 — Your cousin's girlfriend *Hayley*
Needs to promptly admit she judges the whole family silently... *She's not wrong, but we hate her for being right.*

Step 11 — Grandma
She prays daily, but half are passive-aggressive sermons about your tattoos... *Chill Nana.*

Step 12 — Your boss *Gary*
Tries to carry the message... but instead carries the trauma of scheduling 4:30 p.m. *Friday* afternoon meetings about quarterly projections... *Literally, no one cares Gary.*

28

Remember Why You're Here (Hint: It Wasn't For The Spa Amenities)

When you have been in treatment for a while, it is easy to get tunnel vision. You start thinking about that one person who annoys you, the fact that group starts too early, or how you have eaten chicken six nights in a row, just cooked different ways. And if you are not careful, you forget why you walked in here, or why someone had to walk you in.

Nobody comes to rehab because their life was going just fine. You did not wake up one morning perfectly happy and think, "*You know what would be fun? Thirty days of rules and random drug tests.*" You came here because there was a moment, or a whole string of them. The last argument with your family where they slammed the door and said they could not watch you do this anymore. The DUI. The overdose. The "*how did I end up on this stranger's couch*" morning. The money you spent, the custody you risked, the friendships you burned down. That sinking moment when you realized your "*control*" was a total illusion.

You came because something broke. Or maybe everything did. The fight. The job. The trust. The moment you looked in the mirror and did not recognize the person staring back. Or maybe it was the morning you woke up praying not to. Somewhere between "*just one drink*" and "*who the hell pawned my toaster*," things went sideways. Maybe you came because you finally got tired of scaring the people who loved you. Maybe it was because you saw your child standing in the doorway, watching you disappear behind your own eyes.

You are here because somewhere, deep down, a part of you wanted to come back to life. Not just sober, but alive. The kind of alive that looks your kids in the eye again. The kind of alive that remembers what it feels like to mean your own words. Life gave you one more chance, and for reasons you may never understand, you were chosen to take it. You are here because back home was killing you, and this place, this strange, structured, uncomfortable place, is trying to teach you how to live.

Those moments are your why. They are the reason you got past your pride, your fear, or your stubbornness long enough to let someone help you. Remembering them is not about wallowing in guilt. It is about keeping perspective. That truth is what gets you through the worst days here, the days when your mind starts whispering that you are fine. But you remember what fine looked like. Fine was losing everything that mattered and pretending you did not care. Fine was dying with your eyes open.

There will be days in rehab when you forget your why and think about leaving. And when that thought hits, the one that says you could just leave, ask yourself: To do what, exactly? Go get high or drunk? See if you can ruin your life in new and creative ways? Nothing screams "*I have my life together*" like relapse. People who leave AMA think they are walking out strong. No. They are walking out scared. They did not need a getaway car. They needed backbone.

And here is the thing you have to stop pretending: you did not leave a life worth missing. You left wreckage. Nobody begged you not to come here. No one said, "*Please don't go, you are the glue that holds this family together.*" They were more like, "*Pack fast, I already put the directions in Waze.*"

If you start thinking the world wants you back, it doesn't. Do not kid yourself. No one is begging for the old you to come home. They are praying you do not. Even your dog is like, "*We are good, man. Stay as long as you need.*" You did not leave behind adoring fans. Your dealer is not wondering how you are. He moved on. Your old crew is not holding hands singing *Lean on Me*. Nobody is holding a candlelight vigil at the trap house.

And that is okay. Because you are not here to win back the world. You are here to rebuild yourself. You do not have to love rehab. You just have to remember why you needed it. Remember what it cost to get here, who you scared, what you lost, what almost killed you. Because if you forget why you are here, you will forget what happens if you leave too soon.

10 Reasons You're Really Here:

1- That arrest photo where you looked at yourself and said, "*Who's that lady?*"

2- That one ER trip where you tried to charm your way out of a 1013... and failed. (*You flirted, they charted*)

3- Your ex putting "*supervised visits only*" in bold print. ("*Bold? Really?*"...*Always dramatic*)

4- When your mom started hiding her prescriptions in the freezer. (*And you were like, 'Oh, we're playing chess now?'*)

5- That DUI where you blew higher than your GPA.

6- Because even your dealer said, "*Damn, bro, maybe you should chill.*" (*And you asked if that meant he was out or just concerned*)

7- Because your kid learned to check if you were breathing instead of asking for breakfast. (*And that one still stings*)

8- Because your aunt posted "*Please pray*" on *Facebook* and everybody already knew it was about you. (*...and you liked the post*)

9- Because even jail started to feel like a break from real life. (*And the structure? Kinda comforting*)

10- Because your doctor said, "*I don't usually see this in people under 65.*" ... and you're 22. (*And you said, "Wait... is that bad?"*)

29

Proud To Be Here (Because This Is Bravery, Not A Dirty Secret)

Let's get one thing straight: being in treatment is not a shameful thing. *It's brag-worthy.* You didn't sneak into rehab in the middle of the night to hide from the neighbors, you walked *(or maybe crawled)* into the one place that could help you save your own life. That's not weakness. That's guts.

Some people will never understand that. They'll see "*rehab*" and think "*rock bottom*," because they've never had to face their demons head-on. But here's the truth, they might *think* they'd be strong if it were them, but most people don't have the guts to do what you're doing right now.

You're not hiding. You're training. You're in the gym for your soul, building the muscles that will keep you standing when life tries to knock you out again. You're learning things most people never will—like how to sit with your feelings, own your story, and rebuild yourself from the inside out.

And yeah, some folks will talk. Let them. While they're busy whispering about where you've been, you'll be busy building a life you're proud of. And one day, you might even tell your story out loud—not because you owe it to anyone, but because you know it might help someone else be brave, too.

There's no shame in saying, *"I'm in recovery."* The real shame is pretending you don't need it when you do. And you? You didn't just admit you needed help, you showed up for it. That's not stigma-worthy. That's hero-level stuff. Because there's nothing shameful about fighting for your life... and everything powerful about winning.

You're not here because you lost control. You're here because you decided to take it back.

So the next time someone says, *"Oh you went to rehab?"* like its gossip, you look them straight in the eyes and say: *"Yeah and it saved my life."*

And choosing life is the bravest thing a human being can do.

10 Reasons You Should Be Proud to Be in Recovery:

1- You let feelings hit you straight in the face like dodgeballs in middle school gym class — and still showed up for group the next morning.

2- You survived situations that should've required a priest, a lawyer, and a hazmat suit — yet here you are, journaling about gratitude.

3- You've accepted that meetings are forever. Even when you're old, cranky, and smell like mothballs, someone will still be reading *How It Works* in a monotone voice.

4- You've been humbled by rules like *"no hoodies up"* and *"no hugging,"* and still found a way to feel loved anyway.

5- You confessed your wreckage... while *Jennifer* from senior class is still pretending her divorce was *"mutual."*

6- You've had to pee in a cup while someone stared so hard you started wondering if they were trying to summon your ancestors — and you still managed to hit the target.

7- You've seen things that would make a therapist need a therapist — yet somehow you're the one giving advice now.

8- You're giving your future self a fighting chance... and *Future You* is sitting at *Thanksgiving* not as the scandal, but as the one bringing the mac & cheese.

9- You've endured flashlight checks, 6 a.m. vitals, and being treated like you're drug-seeking for asking for *Tylenol.* If that's not mental toughness, I don't know what is.

10- You faced your trauma head-on instead of going on a road trip with no gas money and 3 bench warrants.

30

The Two Times You Need A Meeting (When You Want To Go... And When You Don't)

I used to joke that I went to 547 meetings in rehab, and joke or not, I did not round it. I literally counted every single one. So when I got home and my mother casually asked, "*You are going to a meeting tonight, right?*" I felt irritation shoot through my spine like I was a child being asked if I did my homework. I was a grown woman in my mid-thirties, annoyed simply because she said it. It wasn't that I didn't want recovery. I just didn't want to be parented anymore.

I walked into that meeting like a bratty teenager being forced to go to church. Arms crossed. Sat in the very back. Full "*do not approach me*" body language. I wasn't there to connect or be inspired. I came to silently not participate. If someone had asked how I felt, I probably would have said, *"I want to slam my head in a car door, thanks."*

Then, mid silent tantrum, this man started sharing. Older guy. Hard-working guy. The kind who has carried entire households on his shoulders since he was old enough to lift a toolbox. Work boots still on, laces muddy, jeans stiff like he had just come from a jobsite. There was paint dried into the creases of his knuckles. That was not hobby paint. That was *"my body is my paycheck"* paint. He didn't look like the type to talk about his feelings.

He said that the night before, his wife leaned in to hug him... and he saw her discreetly sniff his breath. He mimicked the tiny head movement, barely noticeable, but it cracked him. He said it hit him hard, because his first instinct was to get offended. Then in the same breath he realized, *"She wasn't trying to catch me. She was trying not to lose me again."* He looked down at his own hands and whispered, *"I put that fear in her."*

And this tough-looking, exhausted, drywall-paint-dust-on-his-knuckles man sobbed. Not cute crying. Not one tear. It was every tear he hadn't been allowed to shed since he was eight years old. He came undone. Right there in that meeting room, he broke open.

Something in my irritation softened. Because that was exactly what my mom was doing when she asked if I was going to a meeting. She wasn't trying to control me. She was checking my breath without checking my breath. She didn't want to bury her daughter.

Addiction does not just destroy the addict. It destroys the family. They paid full price too. They just did not get to numb any of it. And suddenly I wasn't offended anymore. I was humbled. And honestly, I was grateful anyone still wanted me alive enough to even ask.

Then a woman started sharing. First meeting. Younger than me. Her face looked like she had been crying all day, that swollen-eyelid kind of crying. She said earlier that evening her dad knocked on her door because her child had called him saying they were scared. She didn't know what else to do but walk herself into that meeting instead of disappearing into the night. She said, voice barely there, "*I just want to be a mom who doesn't scare her kids anymore.*" That sentence dropped something in me. Because that used to be me. Those early weeks when you don't believe you deserve another chance, but some tiny ember hopes maybe you are wrong. My throat burned, that pre-cry burn, because I knew what it felt like to be the mom your own kids feared. And I never want to be that numb again.

My mind flashed to something that happened a couple weeks earlier. My daughter dropped an entire gallon of milk on the kitchen floor. Milk everywhere. Epic crime scene. She froze and panicked, apologizing like she had destroyed my future. "*Please don't be mad, Mom. Please. I'm sorry. Mom. Please.*" And I laughed and said, "*Baby, it's fine. It's milk. It's not a big deal. We'll clean it up.*" She stared at me like she was looking at a stranger wearing her mother's skin. She said, "*Wow... you really have changed.*" And staring at her nine-year-old little face, I realized I didn't even remember how I used to react. That is how far I had disappeared. My kids had lived in fear of my reactions, and I didn't even remember being that mom.

So when I saw that woman sitting there, terrified her kids would never feel safe around her again, I saw the version of me that existed if one decision went left instead of right.

After that night, I stopped counting meetings and started counting moments. Moments like that father grieving a wife who still loved him but couldn't trust him. Moments like a mother begging the universe for one more chance to be someone her kids felt safe with. And moments like me, realizing these people were not strangers. They were the other versions of me.

That is why you go to meetings. Not just when you want to. Especially when you don't. Because sometimes the night you drag your miserable body into a room you think you cannot stand to be in is the night you remember: I am not the only one trying not to die tonight, and that truth changes everything.

10 Reasons You Should Go to a Meeting:

1- When you want to... because duh, enjoy the rare enthusiasm while it lasts.

2- When you don't... because *"I'm fine"* is addict code for *"I just sniffed a Sharpie to see if it works."*

3- Because it's *Tuesday*... and nothing good has ever happened on a *Tuesday*. Ever.

4- Because the weather is *"partly cloudy"*... and so are all your decisions.

5- Because *Mercury's* in retrograde (*again*)... and apparently so are you.

6- Because your boss said, *"Got a sec?"*... which is corporate for, *"I'm about to ruin your whole day."*

7- Because your kid asked, *"What's for dinner?"*... and your brain answered, *"Fireball shots."*

8- Because *Jim Cantore* showed up in your city... and if the *Weather Channel* guy's here, even the *Universe* is worried about your sobriety.

9- When you say, *"I don't need a meeting today"*... congratulations, you've just written your own relapse obituary. Congrats.

10- Because your ex just texted *"hey stranger"*... and nothing good ever happens after those two words.

31

My Story (From Pills To Pine Straw)

It was a Saturday at noon. Every Saturday at 12:00 p.m. sharp, my dad would pull up outside my best friend's house to pick me up from my sleepover. That was our thing, steady, dependable, sacred in its simplicity. But that day, I wasn't there. At the last minute, I decided to go to *Florida* with my grandmother. I had said no, then yes, then no again, teenage indecision at its finest. Two hours before she left, I caved.

While I was gone, my dad decided to work on the van. Normally he used the four red ramps my grandfather had borrowed the day before. But that day, he used a flimsy jack. It slipped. The van came down. And in one breathless, unthinkable second, my father was gone.

When they told me the time of death, noon, I shattered. The exact moment he should have been pulling into the driveway to get me. I was fourteen and completely certain I had killed my father. Guilt took up residence in me. It became my shadow, louder than grief and sharper than memory.

Two weeks after his funeral, I had a toothache. The dentist gave me *Lorcet*. That first pill did not just numb my jaw; it quieted the part of me that screamed every minute of every day. A few weeks later, I found the half-empty bottle in the kitchen drawer and wondered what would happen if I took a couple just for fun. Twenty-three minutes later, I knew. Warmth. Energy. Relief. For the first time since he died, I smiled without forcing it. That was the day my brain rewired itself.

The next years blurred into bottles and excuses. Migraines. Back pain. Fibromyalgia. Whatever excuse got me another script. *Lorcet*, *Xanax*, *Percocet*, *OxyContin*. *Ambien* became my favorite lullaby. I learned to plan my life around pills, how many I had, how many I needed, how long until the next refill. My calendar was not filled with birthdays or holidays; it was filled with countdowns.

And then came the wreck.

I strapped my baby into a half-buckled car seat and blew through a red light at fifty-five. I hit another car head-on. My head went through the windshield. Sirens. Lights. Blood. Glass. And in the cupholder, four *Ambien* sat like tiny blue witnesses. When I saw the flashing lights, I did what addicts do best: panicked with purpose. I grabbed a greasy *Hardee's* bag, shoved the pills into a half-eaten biscuit, and sealed it shut just before the officer leaned in. They never found them.

A week later, I limped into the junkyard, still bruised and stitched, to see the car. It was mangled and reeking of blood and regret. It looked like a coffin on busted wheels. I reached under the seat, pulled out that same *Hardee's* bag, and unwrapped it. The biscuit was fossilized, but the pills were fine. I swallowed them standing next to the wreck that should have killed me and my child. That was not survival. That was insanity with a pulse.

Eventually the chaos caught up to me. For years, there had been cars parked near my house. When I lived with my ex-husband, I told myself they were land surveyors. Later, when I moved back in with my mom, I convinced myself they were watching the meth house down the road. But they weren't. They were watching me.

The day it came to a head, I went to fill another prescription I had obtained under false pretenses. It was taking too long. Phone calls. Side glances. Then a man in a suit walked in like he had been waiting for this moment. He sat beside me, smiled, and opened a thick folder filled with photos of every driveway my car had been in: my job, my mailbox, my old porch, my mom's porch. Everywhere.

"We've been watching you for three years," he said. For a second, I was flattered. They were the only ones who had been. They thought I was trafficking. I looked him dead in the eye and said, *"You won't find one picture of me handing over a pill to anyone. Every one I ever got, I swallowed, and it still wasn't enough."*

"You need help," he said. *"Put your hands behind your back."*

171

Click.

That night, sitting in a freezing jail cell, something happened I didn't expect: I slept. For the first time in years, I wasn't wired or watching the clock. I just slept. Maybe my body finally surrendered. Maybe it was mercy. Either way, that sleep was grace wearing handcuffs.

When I stood before the judge, I was out of words and out of fight. He looked at me, tired, like he had seen this story a thousand times, and said, *"I can send you to prison for as long as I can, or you can take six months of treatment."*

"I'll have to think about it," I said.

He blinked three times, trying to process what he had just heard. *"Fine,"* he said. *"You've got thirty minutes."*

Outside, my lawyer begged me to say yes. My addict brain tried to reason it out. At least in prison I can get drugs. That is how warped I had become. At twenty-eight minutes, something cracked. *"Okay,"* I whispered. *"I'll go."*

Those two words saved my life.

But saying yes didn't mean I was ready to live. I still had to wait for a bed to open at the only long-term rehab I could afford, and those weeks nearly broke me. By then I was convinced my kids would be better off if my chaos was gone. I had lost everything. I was out on bond, but it didn't feel like freedom. Near the end of my run with pills, it wasn't even life anymore; it was wreckage and heartbreak on repeat. I had lost my husband, my kids, my house, my car, my job, my nursing license, my sanity, even the dog. I was a country song too explicit to play on the radio.

I had been fired from more doctors than most people ever meet. I had nowhere left to hustle, no one left to fool. No one left to lie to or steal from. Every bridge I had ever built was already burned, and I was standing in the smoke with a felony charge pending.

So I sat there thinking, what is the point of being here if I cannot even have the one thing that made life bearable.

That is when I decided to end it.

I swallowed sixty arthritis-strength *Tylenol* in one go, thirty-nine thousand milligrams, hoping my liver would finally do what I couldn't: *quit*. The doctor said he had been in emergency medicine twenty years and had never seen a Tylenol level as high as mine. He leaned over and said, "*You might not make it.*"

I smiled and said, "*Good. That's the plan.*"

Thirteen days in ICU with a sitter, restraints, and a face shield because I was spitting at the nurses. Somehow I was still alive. That is the part I still cannot explain.

It all started with one pill, a *Lorcet*, for a toothache. Eight detoxes, three psych wards, two suicide attempts, and one felony charge later, I finally made it to *Bridges of Hope.* A long-term program for women who had run out of short-term fixes. I walked in half-dead, half-pissed, and fully out of options.

Sixteen women. Timed showers. Chores for everything. No pity. No excuses. No hiding. I cried for two months straight. The women didn't comfort me; they called me out. When I tried to play the victim, they rolled their eyes. When I tried to disappear, they dragged me back. When I said I was different, they laughed and said, "*No, you're not. Sit down.*"

Chores, then chores about chores. Meetings, then meetings about meetings, then meetings about chores. Beds had to be military perfect, tight corners, crisp folds, zero wrinkles, and if not they would flip your bed daily. We bleached bathrooms that were already clean, scrubbed floors until our knees hurt, planted vegetables, and raked pine straw only to re-lay it neater.

Before we laid the pine straw back down, we had to clean it piece by piece. If you have never cleaned pine straw before, just know your arms end up looking like pin cushions. I remember thinking, this must be what losing your mind feels like.

At the time I was pissed. I didn't see how any of it was supposed to help my sobriety. How is picking pine needles therapy. But now, when I get a craving or a trigger, I play my tape back to that exact scene, me sweating, covered in scratches, cleaning pine straw one piece at a time, sitting on a crate in the *Georgia* heat. And then I think, yeah, *no, I'm good.*

That is when it clicks. Ah, this is why. Well played, *Bridges*.

It was like that scene in *The Karate Kid* when he is frustrated painting the fence thinking it is pointless, then later realizes the whole thing was the lesson. That was me. Except my *"paint the fence"* moment was *"clean the straw."*

Somewhere between the bleach and the blisters, something started to change. Every sweep, every scrub, every stupid pine straw poke was scraping away the version of me that did not care anymore.

At *Bridges*, I spent weeks drowning in guilt over what I had done to my kids. I cried every day about the damage, the absence, the shame. One of the women finally looked at me and said, *"Girl, stop crying. You did what you did. If you really love your children, get better, not bitter."*

It hit like a slap and a hug at the same time. Crying over the past didn't make me a better mom. Healing did.

And then there were my resentments, my mom, my ex, everyone I thought had hurt me. I sat there venting, listing every reason I was the way I was, and one of the women stared me down and said, *"Are you a perfect person?"*

"No."

*"Have you hurt people, treated people shi**y, made bad choices?"*

"Yes."

175

"Exactly. People, including you, do shi**y things they shouldn't. They have messed up. You have messed up. We have all messed up. So let it go."

It wasn't said gently, but it landed deep. They were not trying to shame me. They were trying to free me. That is what tough love really is, someone loving you enough to stop agreeing with your pain.

One morning, after another night of crying and bargaining with *God*, I made a deal. If my bed is flipped today, for the sixtieth day in a row, I am leaving. If it is not, I will stay. Prison has to be better than this.

That day, for the first time, my bed was untouched. Later I found out the girl who checked rooms reached for my blanket but then stopped. Something told her to let me slide. The feeling was so overwhelming it shook her. She recalled leaving the room and turning around looking at my messy bed, confused but convinced not to touch it.

That is when I knew *God* had not left me. He had just been waiting for me to show up.

From then on, I stayed. I worked. I told the truth even when it burned. I learned how to feel without using, how to cry without breaking, how to stay when everything in me screamed run. I remember the first time I laughed, a real, ugly, body-shaking laugh. It startled me. It felt foreign and holy at the same time. That is when I knew something was shifting. Little by little, the woman I used to be gave way to the one I was becoming.

Bridges was not just rehab. It was resurrection. That is where I found honesty, humility, and a tiny spark of hope that refused to die. That is where I stopped trying to survive and started learning how to live.

In active addiction, I used to scream at *God*, hitting myself in the head, begging, why did you let all this happen. I never got an answer, *just more pain.*

But a few weeks after I left *Bridges*, I was driving my sister's car because I had nothing. No job. No custody. No plan. Just a borrowed car and a spare room she let me sleep in. *Nickelback* came on the radio, and I started singing, windows down, voice cracking, crying and laughing at the same time. My entire soul felt at peace, at home.

And right in the middle of that mess, I heard it, not out loud, but deep inside: *that is why.*

And I knew.

Because I had to lose everything to find the one thing I never really had, me.

The mom you had isn't coming back. The mom you deserve is.

Addiction didn't destroy me. It stripped me down to truth. It transformed me. *And for that, I am thankful.*

Because I finally understand. I wasn't being punished. I was being led back home to my true self. She had been waiting in

177

the doorway, smiling... like *she knew I would make it.*

32

Apparently I Don't Listen Until Life Throws a Chair

Rehab did not save my life. Rehab handed me a brand-new one and said, "*If you want it, take it.*"

Rehab was the first place I stopped pretending. The first place I stopped managing how I was perceived. The first place I said the things I had been carrying without translating them into humor, silence, or strength. It was the first place I let myself be seen exactly as I was. And for the first time, someone looked back at me and did not see a problem to fix or a failure to judge. They saw someone who was still here. Someone who mattered. Someone worth staying with in the hard moments.

That changed me.

Rehab taught me to stop running from the dark and sit still long enough to realize it was not trying to swallow me. It taught me to put the shovel down. To stop digging. To stop fighting the ground beneath me. That was when it finally clicked. I was never buried. I was planted, even when I could not feel growth happening.

Recovery is the moment the story you have been telling yourself collapses. The moment you understand your past was never a life sentence. It was a syllabus. Every mistake. Every relapse. Every time you stayed somewhere that hurt because leaving felt impossible. Every choice you made just to survive. None of it was wasted. Every part of it was teaching you something about yourself, even when the lesson came wrapped in pain.

The universe was not punishing you. It was trying to reach you. Sometimes the truth does not land until life gets loud enough that you can no longer avoid it. Recovery is when the fog lifts and the truth becomes unavoidable. You are not broken. You are becoming. Shame was never meant to live inside you forever. Guilt was a signal. Regret was a warning. None of them were meant to be your identity.

Your past stops being something you hide from. It stops being a cage. It becomes a map. A reference. A quiet guide that shows you where you have been and reminds you where you do not want to return. And when that shift happens, something inside you finally loosens. You stop punishing yourself for who you were when you did not know another way. You stop dragging your history behind you like proof that you do not deserve what comes next.

You see the truth clearly now. Survival mode was not failure. It was intelligence. It was your body and your soul doing whatever they had to do to keep you alive long enough to reach this moment.

Your past taught you. Your present is healing you. Your future is already waiting, steady and certain, saying, "*You're ready.*" And the version of you walking toward it is no longer carrying every old story like an open wound. You are learning how to move forward without apologizing for having survived.

You do not live in shame anymore. You live in understanding. You do not repeat the same patterns hoping they will hurt less this time. You replace them with choice. You do not carve old pain into your identity. You thank it for what it taught you and you let it go. Your hands are empty now. Your chest can finally expand. There is room inside you for peace. For joy. For a life that does not require constant defense.

That is recovery.

Not fixing yourself. Not erasing your past. Not pretending it did not hurt.

Recovery is choosing to stay. Choosing to live awake. Choosing yourself, again and again, with the full knowledge of where you have been and the quiet certainty that you are worthy of

what comes next.

33

Truth Over Comfort

I have seen what happens when people finally stop running.

I have seen it in myself, and I have seen it in countless others who walked through the doors of rehab carrying shame, exhaustion, and bodies that felt like they could not take another step. These were not weak people. They were people who had been holding everything together for too long, surviving minute by minute, forgetting what it felt like to live without bracing for impact.

In a place that looks ordinary, something extraordinary begins to happen.

Not because pain disappears, and not because anyone fixes you. It happens because the noise finally quiets. The running stops. The constant emergency inside the body slows just enough for the truth to surface.

People begin to stand differently. They breathe more deeply. They laugh again, cautiously at first, as if they are not sure they are allowed to. They start remembering who they were before life taught them to numb, avoid, or self-destruct. I know this because I lived it. Rehab did not just keep me alive. It gave me back a sense of worth I did not realize I had lost.

That kind of change does not come from comfort. It comes from honesty.

Rehab works because it interrupts what is killing you. It replaces chaos with structure, panic with rhythm, and constant reaction with intention. Beige hallways. Quiet rooms. Groups that feel unbearable before they become lifelines. Counselors who stay when you want to push them away. A system that holds you steady when you no longer trust yourself to do it alone.

That is not weakness. That is strength.

Recovery is built in small, human moments that reset something inside you. A meal that tastes like care when nothing else does. A stranger who understands without explanation. A nurse who notices the moment your walls go up. A tech who stays present when your thoughts will not slow down. These moments matter because they prove something essential. You are still human. You are still seen. You are still worth showing up for.

From the outside, rehab does not look dramatic. It looks repetitive. It looks structured. It looks boring. But real transformation is rarely loud. It happens quietly, consistently, in people who keep showing up even when it is uncomfortable, even when it is hard, even when it would be easier to give up.

Rehab is not meant to be polite, and recovery is not meant to be comfortable. If comfort created change, no one would need this process. Comfort keeps people stuck. Comfort protects habits that slowly take lives. Growth requires interruption. Growth requires truth. Growth requires a system strong enough to challenge you and safe enough to hold you at the same time.

People do not change because someone makes them feel better. They change when they finally see clearly. When excuses stop working. When avoidance no longer protects them. When honesty becomes unavoidable and action becomes possible.

Rehab is not designed to be gentle. Recovery is not designed to be easy. They are designed to be real.

And real is what saves lives.

About the Author

Julie Trowell has spent 13 years as a nurse at a nationally recognized addiction treatment center, walking beside patients through their hardest battles. In that time, she's watched hopelessness turn into healing and lives once written off come back to life.

If you've reached this page, maybe you saw yourself somewhere in these words. Maybe you felt a flicker of recognition, or maybe you felt a sting of truth you weren't ready for. Either way—you made it here. And that matters.

I don't know where you are right now—whether you're sitting in a rehab center, hiding in plain sight, or just holding on by a thread—but I need you to hear this: there is still time. Still hope. Still a chance to start again.

If my story proves anything, it's that broken people can rebuild. And maybe—just maybe—the very thing you think disqualifies you is the thing that will set you free.

If you are struggling right now, please don't wait. Call someone. Reach out. Walk through the door. Rehab isn't glamorous, and it won't always feel polite—but it can save your life.

There are people who will listen. There are places that will take you in. And there is still time for you to begin again.

If you or someone you love is struggling with addiction, help is available.:
  - SAMHSA's National Helpline: 1-800-662-HELP (4357)
  - National Suicide Prevention Lifeline: 988
  - Or look up treatment centers in your own community

Media & podcast inquiries:
  therealworldrehab@gmail.com

You can connect with me on:
- http://linkedin.com/in/julie-trowell-803a17109
- https://beacons.ai/therealworldrehab

Made in the USA
Middletown, DE
18 January 2026

27265515R00110